NORWAY'S DELIGHT

DISHES AND SPECIALITIES

Egil Torin Næsheim

NORWAY'S DELIGHT

DISHES AND SPECIALITIES

BY
ELISE SVERDRUP

REVISED EDITION BY
J. AUDREY ELLISON,
B.Sc., F.I.F.S.T.

TANUM – NORLI
OSLO 1980

© ELISE SVERDRUP 1957
Tenth edition 1980
Illustrations by Egil Torin Næsheim

ISBN 82-518-0089-7
Dreyer Aksjeselskap, Stavanger

PREFACE

Almost every nation is renowned for one particular dish which is particularly associated with it, as Sauerkraut is associated with Germany and spaghetti with Italy. China has its Peking duck and Turkey its Turkish delight.

What, then, is Norway's delight? Like the French, we have many. No escargots or grenouilles, but fried cod's tongues and roast sheep's heads and the bonemarrow of reindeer. No pâté de foie gras but «far-reeking», half-fermented trout and sweet, brown goat's-milk cheese. And many other delicious – or surprising – dishes which you may have tasted in Norway and may wish to recreate in your own kitchen.

To make this easy for you this book was written. In the present revised edition a greater degree of precision and clarity in specifying quantities of ingredients has been introduced by adding, where necessary, the metric, British (avoirdupois) and American systems of weights and measures. This has been standardised throughout the book.

For the convenience of those who cook by gas, numbers indicating ovensettings equivalent to temperatures in degrees Celsius/Fahrenheit have been added. Two indices have been appended, one giving English recipe names and the other their Norwegian equivalents, together with a brief glossary of the American equivalents of relevant British culinary terms.

Anyone having difficulty in obtaining suitable ingredients or equipment for preparing the dishes described in this book should get in touch with:

Norway Trade Centre, 20 Pall Mall, London S.W. 1Y 5NE,

or

Scandinavian Suppliers (London) Ltd., 171, Ilderton Road, London, S.E. 16,

or

The Export Council of Norway, 800 Third Avenue, New York, N.Y. 10022, USA.

London, June 1980

J. Audrey Ellison

CONTENTS

Local Specialities

ARENDAL CAKES Arendalskaker

3 eggs
175 g | 6 oz | ¾ cup sugar
90 g | 3 oz | ¾ cup flour
2 tablespoons blanched almonds
¼ teaspoon baking powder

Whisk two egg yolks and one whole egg with sugar, add flour and baking powder. Spoon dough with a teaspoon on to a greased tin, and decorate with almond halves. Bake for 12 minutes in a moderately slow oven (Mark 3: 170° C/325° F). Makes 40.

CURED MUTTON RIBS FROM BERGEN Bergensk pinnekjøtt

1½ kg | 3 lb mutton ribs
2 tablespoons salt
1 tablespoon sugar
½ teaspoon saltpetre

Rub seasoning into meat. Dry ribs, and hang three days in an airy place. Crush bones, place ribs in a very hot oven (Mark 8: 230° C/450° F). After 15 minutes pour over 40 cl | ¾ pint | 2 cups boiling water. Baste every 10 minutes. If the meat gets too dry, cover with greaseproof paper for the last half hour. Roasting time: 1½–2 hours. Serve with mashed swedes. A Christmastime delicacy from western Norway.
The name "pinnekjøtt" comes from the old method of preparing this dish. At the bottom of a cauldron was placed a small quantity of thin birch twigs. The meat was placed on the twigs, and steam roasted. Serves 6.

9

BERGEN TWISTS Bergenskringler

*250 g | ½ lb | 2 cups
flour
40 g | 1½ oz | 3 table-
spoons butter
¼ l | ⅜ pint | 1 cup
tepid milk
20 g | ¾ oz fresh yeast or
1 tablespoon dried yeast
or 1 yeast cake*

Cream the yeast with a little tepid milk and mix the rest of the milk with the melted butter. Pour the creamed yeast and the liquid into the flour and mix to a firm dough. Put the dough in a warm place to rise for 20 to 30 minutes and knead once during proving. Shape the dough into little-finger-sized pieces. Do not use dusting flour, but moisten the hands with tepid water. Form into B-shaped twists and boil in a large pan of unsalted water for 5 minutes. The twists will rise to the surface when they are ready and doubled in size. Lift out using a perforated spoon and place on a baking sheet. Bake at Mark 6: 200° C/400° F for 15 minutes until golden brown. Reduce the heat to Mark ½: 130° C/250° F and let the twists dry until crisp.
Serve with butter and cured meats. Makes 25.

POLAR BEAR'S EYE Isbjørnøye

*60 g | 2 oz finely chopped
parsley
8 sliced and cleaned
anchovies
1 finely chopped boiled
potato
4 tablespoons of raw
chopped onion
1 boiled finely chopped
beetroot
4 yolks of egg*

Make a circle on each plate of chopped parsley, anchovies, potatoes, onion and beetroot. Pour the raw yolks of egg carefully into the middle, and serve with flatbread and a pat of butter. Serves 4.

DRAMMEN CREAM CAKES Drammensfløtekaker

40 cl | 3/4 pint | 2 cups
double cream
3 eggs
4 tablespoons castor
sugar
125 g | 4 oz | 1 cup flour
1 teaspoon baking
powder

Whip cream until stiff, beat eggs and sugar until thick, and mix. Add flour and baking powder to make a dough. Grease a number of small cake tins well with butter, fill three-quarters full with dough. Dry cakes in very slow oven (Mark 1/4: 120° C/225° F), and do not open oven door for first half hour. Dry the cakes – do not bake them – until they are pale gold, light, and crisp. Makes 30.

FEVIG MACKEREL Fevig makrell

4 mackerel
6 potatoes
1 bunch chives
125 g | 4 oz | 1/2 cup
butter

Clean fish, peel and slice potatoes, chop chives. Put the fish, potatoes, and chives in layers in a greased fireproof dish. Dot with pats of butter and bake in a moderately hot oven (Mark 4: 180° C/350° F) for 40 minutes. Serves 6.

HALLINGDAL SOUR-CREAM BREAD Hallingdal rømmebrød

1/4 l | 3/8 pint | 1 cup sour
cream
175 g | 6 oz | 3/4 cup
margarine
2 potatoes
Sufficient plain flour to
make a firm dough
a little castor sugar

Grate the potatoes finely. Knead the cold margarine. Beat in the flour and sour cream alternately to make a soft, smooth dough. The dough stiffens on being chilled. Knead the dough together and shape into a thick "sausage". Cover the dough carefully and set aside in a cold place overnight. Roll out the dough very thinly. Sprinkle with the castor sugar and roll the sugar into the dough. Bake in a moderate oven (Mark 4: 180° C/350° F) until golden brown and crisp. Serve with coffee.

BERGEN PRESSED COD Persetorsk

Cut the head off a large cod (2 kg | 4 lb) and cut the fish down the back. Wash and rub in a pinch of salt, and then place in a vessel sprinkled with salt for four days.

Remove the fish, rinse, and press between two broad boards, with a stone on top. Allow the fish to soak in water for one day, and boil in unsalted water. Serve with mustard sauce. Serves 8.

GEILO DESSERT Geilodessert

8 slices sponge cake
1/4 l | 3/8 pint | 1 cup cloud-berries
1/4 l | 3/8 pint | 1 cup double cream, whipped
1 tablespoon sugar

On each dessert plate place one slice of cake, covered with cloudberries. Place the other piece of cake on top, and decorate with a spoonful of sweetened whipped cream and a few choice berries. Serves 4.

GRIMSTAD RUSKS Grimstadkavringer

750 g | 1 1/2 lb | 6 cups flour
250 g | 1/2 lb | 1 cup sugar
250 g | 1/2 lb | 1 cup butter
4 teaspoons baking powder
40 cl | 3/4 pint | 2 cups cream

Mix all the ingredients into a dough and form into fifty rusks. Bake in a moderately hot oven (Mark 5: 190° C/375° F), then split quickly across with a sharp knife. Dry in very slow oven (Mark 1/4: 120° C/225° F) until golden and crisp. Makes 100 rusks.

HALLINGDAL BANNOCKS Hallingdallefser

A bannock is a soft flatbread, baked on a girdle, which should be quickly wrapped in a clean cloth, to keep it soft. It should be served buttered. In some parts of Norway people like to sprinkle sugar on it, others prefer goat's-milk cheese on their bannock. The bannock should be served rolled up into a cone shape.

HAUGESUND PICKLED HERRINGS Haugesunds sildesalat

2 large salted herrings
2 tablespoons vinegar
2 tablespoons oil
1 teaspoon pepper
3 tablespoons sugar
1 finely chopped pickled
beetroot
chopped parsley
1 small finely chopped
onion

Dress the herrings and soak them for twelve hours. Cut into oblique pieces, 2,5 cm (one inch) long, and place on a flat dish so that the herrings look intact. Stir together oil, vinegar, sugar, and pepper, pour over herrings. Set aside in a cool place for three hours. Decorate with chopped onion, beetroot and parsley. Serve with freshly boiled potatoes and a large bowl of thick sour cream. Serves 4.

HARDANGER: MOTHER UTNE'S COFFEE CAKE   Mor Utnes kaffekake fra Hardanger

250 g | ½ lb | 1 cup butter or margarine
500 g | 1 lb | 2 cups sugar
250 g | ½ lb | 2 cups flour
1 teaspoon baking powder
2 eggs
¼ l | ⅜ pint | 1 cup milk
grated rind of one lemon

Cream the butter and sugar until white, add flour, milk and eggs alternately. Bake in a greased floured tin in a moderately hot oven (Mark 4: 180° C/350° F) for 60 minutes, and cover with lemon icing. Makes one cake.

TRONDHEIM SOUP Trondhjemssuppe

90 g | 3 oz | ½ cup rice
150 g | 5 oz | 1 cup raisins
¼ l | ⅜ pint | 1 cup sour cream
2 tablespoons sugar
1½ l | 2½ pints | 6 cups water
¼ l | ⅜ pint | 1 cup raspberry juice
½ lemon

Rinse rice and boil 30 minutes. Add raisins, and boil another 15 minutes. Whip cream with sugar until stiff, add fruit juice and grated lemon. Pour into soup, stirring vigorously. The pale pink soup can be served tepid or cold, with a spoonful of cream on it. Serves 6.

LOFOTEN CAVIAR Lofotkaviar

500 g | 1 lb fresh cod's roe 1 tablespoon salt 1/4 teaspoon saltpetre 1/4 l | 3/8 pint | 1 cup vegetable oil 1 tablespoon sugar 1/2 teaspoon salt	Remove all skin from roe, stir with salt and saltpetre and allow to stand one day. Stir in oil, salt and sugar and mix to a smooth mass. Put into small jars. Pour a teaspoonful of oil on top of each. Ready for use after eight days.

AALESUND BROTH Ålesund brennesnute – betagryn

500 g | 1 lb salted meat, minced 4 medium-sized potatoes 90 g | 3 oz | 1/2 cup dried yellow peas salt pepper parsley 90 g | 3 oz | 1/2 cup fresh peas 2 carrots 1/2 stick of celery (or 30 g | 1 oz celeriac) 1 leek 90 cl | 1 1/2 pints | 4 cups water	Soak peas and meat for twenty-four hours. Bring the peas, meat, and water to the boil, then cook for three hours. Add sliced potatoes and vegetables, allow to simmer another hour for a soup of thick consistency. Serves 6.

OSLO SWEET SOUP Oslo fruktsuppe

60 g | 2 oz | 1/2 cup rolled oats 90 cl | 1 1/2 pints | 4 cups water 150 g | 6 oz | 1 cup prunes 1/4 l | 3/8 pint | 1 cup strong fruit juice 2 tablespoons sugar	Leave the prunes to soak in water for one day. Boil the rolled oats, the water, and the prunes for an hour, add the juice and sugar, and serve with small, home-made rusks. Serves 4.

Porridges and Soups

"Can you make porridge?" – "No." – "Then you may as well pack up," they say in Telemark, to emphasise the fact that a woman who cannot make porridge is useless. In former times porridge was our native staple dish, and an old proverb says that 'porridge has fed more people than it has ever killed".

BERNT BALCHEN'S SOUP Bernt Balchens suppe

4 large potatoes
2 onions
1/2 root of celeriac
40 cl | 3/4 pint | 2 cups water
90 cl | 1 1/2 pints | 4 cups milk
1 tablespoon cold butter
salt
pepper

Clean vegetables, and chop up finely. Place in saucepan with water and boil for 30 minutes. Add salt and pepper. Pour on milk. Bring the soup once more to boil, add butter. Serves 6.

VEGETABLE BROTH Brennesnute

1/2 root of celeriac
1 carrot
1 leek
1 potato
2 l | 3 1/4 pints | 2 quarts good stock
2 1/2 tablespoons butter
2 tablespoons flour
salt and pepper
plenty of chopped parsley

Clean vegetables, cut into fine strips, and boil in the stock until soft. Brown butter, add flour and a little stock, and allow to simmer for five minutes. Add salt, then the vegetables and stock, adjust seasoning, sprinkle with parsley, and serve piping hot on a cold winter's day. Serves 6.

BROWN FISH SOUP Brun fiskesuppe

1/2 onion
1/4 root of celeriac
1 chopped leek
2 carrots
1 1/2 l | 2 1/2 pints | 1 1/2
quarts fish stock
1 rasher bacon
2 tablespoons tomato
purée
2 tablespoons butter
1 tablespoon flour
1 glass sherry
a few small fishballs

Clean vegetables, cut up and boil in fish stock with the bacon until tender. Strain soup and add tomato purée. Brown butter and flour, add the stock, and allow to simmer for five minutes. Add the salt, sherry, and a few small fishballs. Serves 6.

BUTTERMILK SOUP Kjernemelksuppe

2 yolks of egg
4 tablespoons sugar
1/4 l | 3/8 pint | 1 cup
(double) cream
90 cl | 1 1/2 pints | 1 quart
buttermilk

Whisk together the yolks of egg and the sugar until white, whip the cream and add. Pour cold buttermilk into the cream, and serve. Serves 4.

CARAWAY SOUP Karvekålsuppe

2 tablespoons butter
1 1/2 tablespoons flour
1/4 l | 3/8 pint | 1 cup
finely chopped fresh car-
away sprouts
90 cl | 1 1/2 pints | 1 quart
good veal stock
1/4 l | 3/8 pint | 1 cup
coarsely chopped caraway
sprouts
1 teaspoon salt
1 yolk of egg
2 tablespoons cream

Melt butter with flour and finely chopped caraway sprouts. Add stock, allow to simmer five minutes. Add salt, then coarsely chopped caraway sprouts. Remove saucepan, whisk together the egg yolk and cream and pour into the hot soup. Garnish with poached eggs or slices of hard-boiled egg. Serve buttered toast with the soup. This is the supreme springtime soup. Serves 4.

CREAM PORRIDGE, OUR NATIONAL DISH Rømmegrøt

40 cl | ¾ pint | 2 cups
thick sour cream
90 cl | 1½ pints | 1 quart
milk
125 g | 4 oz | 1 cup flour
½ teaspoon salt

Boil cream for five minutes. Sprinkle in four tablespoons flour, beat porridge until butter oozes out. Skim off butter with a tablespoon and keep hot. Add remaining flour, pour on the rest of the boiling milk. Boil for five minutes to a smooth consistency. Add salt. Pour into hot soup plates, pour over a little melted butter. Serve with sugar, cinnamon, and fruit juice, and aquavit for a special occasion. Serves 6.

RICE PORRIDGE Risengrynsgrøt

1½ l | 2½ pints | 6 cups
milk
125 g | 4 oz | ½ cup rice
1 teaspoon salt

Rinse rice several times, boil the milk, sprinkle rice into it slowly, and allow porridge to simmer for an hour. Add salt. Serve with a pat of butter in the middle, sugar, and cinnamon, and a jug of fruit juice diluted with water. Rice porridge is a traditional Christmas Eve dish in Norway, and to this day in many parts of Norway the farmer's wife puts a plateful of rice porridge in the barn for the 'julenisse' – Norway's own little gnome of a Father Christmas. Serves 4.

DANCING MASTER'S SOUP Dansemestersuppe

1½ l | 2½ pints | 1½
quarts fruit juice and water
1½ tablespoons potato
flour
sugar
8 small rusks

Boil fruit juice and water, add a mixture of potato flour stirred in a little cold water. Bring quickly to boil, add sugar to taste. Serve cold with small rusks. Serves 4.

BOILED FRESH BEEF AND SOUP Ferskt kjøtt og suppe

1½ kg | 3 lb beef
3 l | 5 pints | 3 quarts
cold water
2 tablespoons salt
2 carrots
1 parsnip
2 leeks
pepper and salt
Sauce:
2 tablespoons butter
1 tablespoon flour
40 cl | 1¼ pints | 3 cups
meat stock
1 tablespoon sugar
1 tablespoon vinegar
2 tablespoons grated
horse-radish

Wash meat and place in saucepan with cold water. Bring to boil. Skim carefully, allow meat to boil two hours. Add clean chopped vegetables, boil for another thirty minutes. Add pepper and salt. Melt butter and flour, add meat stock, simmer for five minutes, add seasoning. Serve the soup first. The meat is served as a separate dish, with potatoes and horse-radish sauce. This is typical Norwegian he-man's fare.

NORWEGIAN FISH SOUP Fiskesuppe

1 tablespoon flour
2 tablespoons butter
1½ l | 2½ pints | 1½
quarts fish stock
1 tablespoon finely chopped chives
2 tablespoons sour cream
12 small fishballs
salt

Melt butter with flour, slowly add hot stock and allow to simmer five minutes. Add salt, remove saucepan from the heat and add the chives and cream. A few small fishballs and a little pickled purslane or pickled marrow may be added to taste. Serves 6.

PEA SOUP WITH PORK Gul ertesuppe

500 g | 1 lb dried yellow
peas
3 l | 5 pints | 3 quarts
boiling water
500 g | 1 lb salt lean pork
1 carrot
1 leek
½ root of celeriac

Soak peas for 24 hours. Put into boiling water, add pork and vegetables, allow to simmer until peas are quite soft. Serve soup together with pork. Small meatballs and potatoes browned in sugar may be added. Serves 8.

NORWEGIAN ALE SOUP Ølsuppe

40 cl | ³/₄ pint | 2 cups
ale or beer
90 cl | 1 ½ pints | 4 cups
water
2 yolks of egg
2 tablespoons cream
1 tablespoon sugar
8 tablespoons | ½ cup
crisply toasted cubes of
white bread

Beat ale, water, eggs, and cream in saucepan and bring to boil. Add the sugar. Stir constantly. Garnish with toast cubes. Serves 4.

NAIL SOUP Spikersuppe

8 potatoes
4 leeks
1 ½ l | 2 ½ pints | 6 cups
water
3 tablespoons butter
salt and pepper

Clean and slice potatoes, and boil to a soft mash. Clean leeks, cut into long strips, and boil with the soup for 15 minutes. Add seasoning and butter. A cheap and tasty everyday soup. Serves 4.

Fish

Innumerable varieties of fish are available in Norway. Fish is served almost daily in many homes in this country. When properly cooked it is delicious, nutritious, economical and easily digested.
Whether the Norwegian housewife prepares the Saturday herring or an elaborate aspic dish she uses imagination and adds small finishing touches to the meals she serves.

FRIED COLEY Seibiff

1 kg | 2 lb fresh coley (also known as saithe or coalfish)
1 teaspoon salt
1/4 teaspoon pepper
2 tablespoons flour
2 onions

Clean fish. Boil head, skin and bones to make stock for sauce. Cut fish into large pieces, coat with mixture of flour and salt, fry and season. Serve with lots of fried onions and sauce made from strained and reduced stock. Add a little cream and a few drops of caramelised sugar to the sauce. Serves 6.

FINNAN HADDIE (Smoked Haddock) Røket kolje

1 kg | 2 lb haddock
1 tablespoon salt
1 1/2 l | 2 1/2 pints | 6 cups water
carrots
chopped parsley
2 hard-boiled eggs
250 g | 1/2 lb | 1 cup butter

Skin fish and cut in pieces. Boil 10 minutes in salted water. Serve with boiled, diced carrots and chopped parsley. Cream butter, add finely chopped eggs and serve with the fish. Serves 4.

26

BOILED COD Kokt torsk

1 large cod | 2 to 2¹/₂
kg | 4 to 5 lb
90 cl | 1¹/₂ pints | 4 cups
water
250 g | ¹/₂ lb | 1 cup salt
1 tablespoon vinegar
1 sprig seaweed (optional)

Clean fish without cutting open. Cut into 2¹/₂ cm | 1 inch slices. Put under running water, cover with a few ice cubes. Bring water, salt and vinegar to a brisk boil. Put in fish, head, liver and roe as soon as the water boils and allow to simmer for 4 to 5 minutes. Skim carefully. In the southern part of Norway it is customary to add a sprig of seaweed to the water. It brings out the fine iodine flavour. Serve fish piping hot with freshly boiled potatoes and creamed butter mixed with finely chopped parsley. Mustard, vinegar, pepper and thin rye crispbread may accompany this dish. Serves 6.

A paradox: In Norway claret is served with boiled cod.

COD'S ROE Torskerogn

500 g | 1lb fresh cod's
roe
90 cl | 1¹/₂ pints | 4 cups
water
2 teaspoons salt
1 lemon
125 g | 4 oz | ¹/₂ cup
butter

Wrap roe in cheesecloth and boil for 30 minutes in salted water. Cool. Slice, coat with flour and fry in butter until golden brown. Serve with wedges of lemon. Serves 4.
Cod's roe, hot or cold, makes a delicious sandwich spread.

FRIED MACKEREL Stekt makrell

4 mackerel
1 teaspoon salt
2 tablespoons flour
4 tablespoons butter
parsley

Clean fish and dry well. Coat with mixture of flour and salt, fry in butter until golden brown. Garnish with crisply fried parsley. Serves 4.

LYE FISH Lutefisk

1 kg | 2 lb lye fish (see below)
90 cl | 1 1/2 pints | 4 cups water
60 g | 2 oz | 1/4 cup salt

Cut fish in large pieces, simmer for 1 minute in unsalted water, add salt and simmer for another 5 minutes. The addition of salt after fish has come to the boil gives it the right consistency and a fine flavour. Serve with freshly boiled potatoes, stewed yellow split peas, melted butter or drippings from roast pork.

Lye fish is a traditional Christmas dish in Norway. Serves 4.

How to prepare Lye Fish in three easy steps:

1. Soak fish in water 2 to 3 days. Change water frequently.
2. Skin fish and cure in lye mixture 2 to 3 days (12 1/2 l | 10 quarts | 12 1/2 U.S. quarts | water to 1 1/4 l | 1 quart | 5 cups lye).
3. Soak in cold water 2 to 3 days. Change water frequently.

Lye fish is made of dried cod.

FISH AU GRATIN Fiskegrateng

250 g | 1/2 lb | 1 1/4 cups boiled fish, skinned and boned
60 g | 2 oz | 4 table-spoons butter
3 tablespoons flour
3/4 l | 1 1/4 pints | 3 cups milk
4 eggs, separated
1/2 teaspoon salt
1/4 teaspoon pepper
1 tablespoon sherry
breadcrumbs

Melt butter, stir in flour. Add milk gradually, then egg yolks and flaked fish. Season and add wine. Beat egg whites until stiff. Fold in. Grease baking dish, coat with fine breadcrumbs. Pour in mixture. Bake in a moderate oven (Mark 5: 190° C/375° F) 45 minutes. Serves 4.

CREAMED COD Plukkfisk

350 g | ¾ lb | 2 cups
boiled cod, skinned and
boned
5–6 large boiled potatoes
1 tablespoon flour
2 tablespoons butter
¾ l | 1¼ pints | 3 cups
milk
1 teaspoon salt
½ teaspoon pepper
1 large bunch chives

Cut potatoes in small pieces, flake the fish. Make thick white sauce, season, stir in fish and potatoes. Bring to the boil. Sprinkle generously with chopped chives. Delicious with thin rye crispbread and butter. Serves 4.

POUNDED FISH Fiskefarse

1 kg | 2 lb finely minced
fish, preferably haddock
2 teaspoons salt
2 tablespoons flour
2 tablespoons potato flour
or cornflour
125 g | 4 oz | ½ cup
butter
⅛ teaspoon nutmeg
¼ teaspoon pepper
90 cl | 1½ pints | 4 cups
cold, boiled milk
¼ l | ⅜ pint | 1 cup cold,
boiled cream

Beat fish and salt for 15 minutes to make a light soft mixture. Add flour, potato flour and cold butter. Season. Add milk and cream gradually. Make into steamed fish pudding (see Fish Aspic), fishballs poached in fish stock, or fried fish cakes.

JANSSON'S TEMPTATION Janssons fristelse

4 raw potatoes
8 fillets of anchovy
1 chopped onion
¼ l | ⅜ pint | 1 cup
cream
2 tablespoons butter

Put layers of sliced potatoes, fillets of anchovy, and onion fried in butter into a greased baking dish. Pour over cream, dot with butter. Bake the "temptation" in a hot oven (Mark 6: 200° C/400° F) for 45 minutes. Serve piping hot. Serves 4.

29

GLAZIER'S HERRING Glassmestersild

2 large salt herrings
1/2 sliced onion
1 teaspoon peppercorns
1/2 teaspoon sugar
4 bay leaves
Marinade:
1/4 l | 3/8 pint | 1 cup distilled vinegar
1/4 l | 3/8 pint | 1 cup water
4 tablespoons sugar
fresh dill

Clean, skin, bone and fillet fish. Soak in cold water for 12 hours. Cut in slices of about 1 cm | 1/2 inch. Arrange in layers with onion, bay leaves and peppercorns, add sugar. Boil marinade, cool and pour over fish. Sprinkle with fresh dill. Ready to use in 3 days.

TOMATO-HERRING SALAD Tomatsild

3 salt herrings
70 g | 2 1/4 oz | 3 tablespoons tomato paste
2 chopped onions
12 bay leaves
2 tablespoons sugar
4 tablespoons distilled vinegar
1 tablespoon water

Clean herrings and soak for 6 hours in cold water. Cut in small pieces. Blend seasoning, tomato paste and water. Marinate herring in mixture. Allow to stand for 48 hours before use.

OLSEN'S DREAM DISH Olsens drømmerett

4 fresh herrings
4 anchovy fillets, finely chopped
2 tablespoons Norwegian caviar
8 tablespoons | 1/2 cup fine breadcrumbs
salt
pepper
1 tablespoon chilled butter
1 glass sherry

Clean and fillet fish. Cover each fillet with a layer of anchovy and caviar. Roll and fasten with toothpick. Coat with breadcrumbs. Pack tightly together in buttered baking dish. Dot with butter, pour over wine. Bake 30 minutes in a moderate oven (Mark 5: 190° C/375° F). Serves 4.

FISH ASPIC Fiskekabaret (For Special Occasions)

500 g | 1 lb minced fish 150 g | 5 oz | 1 cup prawns, lobster or mussels 250 g | 1/2 lb | 1 cup Italian salad (mixed vegetable mayonnaise) 40 to 75 cl | 3/4 to 1 3/4 pints | 3 to 4 cups light aspic jelly or 2 tablespoons | 2 envelopes gelatine powder 250 g | 1/2 lb | 1 cup petits pois parsley 1 tube mayonnaise	Steam minced fish in a well greased, round baking dish for 1 hour. Cool. Cut pudding in two lengthwise. Cover one layer with Italian salad, prawns, lobster or mussels. Place second layer on top. Coat with light aspic jelly or gelatine dissolved in cooled water and seasoned to taste. Before gelatine is completely set decorate top with the peas and prawns. Chill 2 hours. Place on a round serving dish. Decorate with mayonnaise. Cut in wedges. Serve with mayonnaise, fresh rolls and pats of butter. Serves 4–6.

BOILED TROUT Kokt ørret

1 trout (1/2 to 1 kg | 1 to 2 lb) 3/4 l | 1 1/4 pints | 3 cups water 1/4 l | 3/8 pint | 1 cup vinegar 2 tablespoons salt 1 lemon 125 g | 4 oz | 1/2 cup butter 1 bunch parsley	Clean fish. Bring water, salt and vinegar to the boil. Add fish. Remove from heat and allow to stand for 15 to 20 minutes according to size. Serve on a hot oblong dish. Garnish with sprigs of parsley and wedges of lemon. Cream butter, mix with finely chopped parsley and serve with fish. Serves 4.

MOUNTAIN TROUT Fjellørret

4 small trout 1 tablespoon salt 2 tablespoons flour 3 tablespoons butter slices of lemon parsley	Clean, wash and dry fish. Coat with mixture of flour and salt. Fry in butter until golden brown. Serve with slices of lemon, garnish with parsley. Serves 4.

CORNED TROUT Rakørret

trout, freshly caught
salt
sugar
water

A ½ to 1 kg | 1 to 2 lb fish is a good size for corning. Clean, sprinkle head and belly with salt. Arrange in a wooden container, belly-side upwards. Sprinkle salt and 1 teaspoon sugar between each layer of fish and weigh each layer down with something heavy to extract the liquid. Liquid should cover fish completely. Ready to use in about 3 months. Serve very cold with thin rye crispbread and butter. Beer and aquavit are essential with this lordly repast.

Ovnskokt kveite
BAKED FISH (100-year-old recipe from Southern Norway.)

1 kg | 2 lb halibut, skin-
ned and boned
125 g | 4 oz | ½ cup but-
ter
2 tablespoons flour
35 cl | ⅝ pint | 1½ cups
of fish stock
8 tablespoons | ½ cup
cream
1 teaspoon salt
2 egg yolks
½ teaspoon pepper
1 tablespoon fresh lemon
juice
2 tablespoons sherry

Boil skin and bones to make stock. Cut fish in small pieces. Coat with flour and fry until golden brown. Arrange in baking dish, sprinkle with lemon juice, salt and pepper. Make brown gravy from butter, flour and fish stock, pour over fish. Bake in a hot oven (Mark 6: 200° C/400° F) 25 to 30 minutes. Add wine. Serve in baking dish. Serves 6.

SMOKED SALMON Røket laks

Smoked salmon is best when mildly cured. Slice thinly and serve with scrambled eggs or creamed spinach. Smoked salmon and corned trout are considered delicacies by connoisseurs.

BOILED SALMON Kokt laks

1 kg | 2 lb fresh salmon,
cut in slices
250 g | 1/2 lb | 1 cup salt
3³/4 l | 6¹/2 pints | 1 gal-
lon water

Bring water to the boil. Add fish and allow to simmer 12 to 15 minutes. Skim carefully to prevent a grey film from forming on the pink flesh. Serve salmon on a hot dish. Garnish with parsley and lemon wedges. Very tasty with Hollandaise sauce or creamed butter with chopped parsley. Serves 6.

COLD SALMON Kokt laks, kald (A dish fit for a king)

1 kg | 2 lb salmon
4 hard-boiled eggs
4 tomatoes
150 g | 5 oz | 1 cup peel-
ed prawns
2 heads lettuce
1 cucumber
1 bunch parsley
mayonnaise

Boil salmon, skin and bone carefully. Cool in stock. Serve on a round dish on a bed of crisp lettuce leaves and sliced cucumber. Garnish with eggs, tomatoes and parsley. Cover with mayonnaise, sprinkle with fresh dill and prawns. Serve extra mayonnaise separately.
To vary: Substitute halibut or trout for salmon. Delicious and more economical. Serves 8.

LOBSTER A LA KING Hummer à la king (For special guests)

2 large lobsters
2 tablespoons butter
2 tablespoons flour
1/4 l | 3/8 pint | 1 cup
cream
125 g | 4 oz | 1 cup
mushrooms, sliced
2 egg yolks
1 glass sherry
15 g | 1/2 oz | 1/2 cup fine
breadcrumbs

Boil lobsters, cool and cut in two. Crack claws. Remove meat carefully. Make white sauce of butter, flour and cream. Season. Add lobsters cut in pieces, mushrooms, egg yolks and wine. Return to shell, dot with butter and sprinkle with crumbs. Bake for 15 minutes in a hot oven (Mark 6: 200° C/400° F). Serve hot with toast and butter. Serves 4.

33

LOBSTER NATUREL Hummer naturell

2 lobsters
3³/₄ l | 6¹/₂ pints | 1 gallon water
250 g | ¹/₂ lb | 1 cup salt
1 tablespoon sugar

Bring water, salt and sugar to the boil. Plunge one lobster at a time into rapidly boiling water, head first. Quickly cover with a lid. Bring water to a brisk boil again before adding the second lobster. Boil 15 to 20 minutes, according to size. Cool in water. Cut lobsters in two, lengthwise. Remove stomach or "lady", a small sack just behind the eyes. Crack claws. Arrange on dish, garnish with wedges of lemon, parsley and crisp lettuce leaves. Serve with mayonnaise or French dressing and toast and butter. Serves 4.

Meat

MEAT ROAST VEAL Kalvestek

Joint of veal 3 kg | 6–7 lb
2 teaspoons salt
1 teaspoon pepper
40 cl | 3/4 pint | 2 cups
boiling water or milk
1/4 l | 3/8 pint | 1 cup sour
cream
1 tablespoon butter
gravy browning

Wash and dry the joint, rub with butter, salt and pepper, and place in a hot oven, kept at Mark 8: 230° C/ 450° F for half an hour. Then baste the joint with milk or water every 10 minutes. Roast for a further 1 1/2 hours in a moderate oven (Mark 4: 180° C/ 350° F). Remove the joint, pour off the gravy, and return the joint to the oven for 5 minutes in order to make it crisp on the outside. Reduce the gravy, adding cream, a pat of butter, 1 tablespoon water, and the gravy browning. Serve with boiled vegetables, lettuce, and cucumber. Serves 6–8.

SAILOR'S STEW Sjømannsbiff

500 g | 1 lb beef
3 tablespoons flour
2 teaspoons salt
6 large potatoes
4 carrots
1 large onion
4 tomatoes
1 teaspoon salt
1/2 teaspoon pepper
60 cl | 1 pint | 2 1/2 cups
boiling water

Cut meat in slices, cover with flour and salt mixture. Brown. Dice potatoes, carrots, onion and tomatoes. Arrange layers of meat and vegetables in casserole, add seasoning and water and simmer over a low heat under a tight lid for about 2 hours. Serves 4.

BEEF OLIVES Benløse fugler

8 slices beef, trimmed
1 teaspoon salt
1/2 teaspoon pepper
250 g | 1/2 lb forcemeat
75 g | 2 1/2 oz | 5 table-
spoons butter
40 cl | 3/4 pint | 2 cups
meat stock

Clean meat, dry and pound flat. Sprinkle with salt and pepper. Place 1 tablespoon forcemeat on each slice, roll and fasten with string. Brown in butter. Make brown gravy with flour and butter, add hot meat stock and simmer the rolls in gravy for 20 to 25 minutes. Serve with red whortleberry or cranberry relish, pickles and fried potatoes. Serves 4.

MUTTON AND CABBAGE STEW Fårikål (Traditional Norwegian dish)

1 kg | 2 lb mutton
1 kg | 2 lb cabbage
1 head Savoy cabbage
3/4 l | 1 1/4 pints | 3 cups
boiling water
2 teaspoons salt
10 black peppercorns
1 tablespoon chopped
parsley

Wash meat and cut in pieces. Parboil cabbage and slice. Arrange meat and cabbage in layers, putting fat pieces of meat in the bottom of the sauce-pan. Sprinkle with salt. Tie the pep-percorns in a small piece of cheese-cloth and boil with the meat. Allow to simmer under a tight lid for 2 hours, add Savoy cabbage cut in slices and cook 1/2 hour more. Sprinkle with parsley and serve. Gourmets prefer this dish when warmed up 3 times. Remember piping hot plates for each serving. Serves 6.

LEFTOVER MEAT DISH Pytt i panne

500 g | 1 lb | 1 1/2 cups
leftover meat
4 boiled potatoes
8 tablespoons | 1/2 cup
leftover gravy
pinch of pepper
4 eggs
1/2 teaspoon salt

Cut meat and potatoes in very small pieces. Heat in gravy in a frying pan. Add seasoning. Just before serving pour one egg per person carefully over meat. Cook over a low heat until the eggs are firm. Serves 4.

MEATBALLS Kjøttkaker

500 g | 1 lb minced beef
15 g | 1/2 oz | 1/2 cup
breadcrumbs
1 egg, beaten
1/2 teaspoon salt
pinch of pepper
2 tablespoons butter
2 tablespoons flour
40 cl | 3/4 pint | 2 cups
meat stock

Blend meat, crumbs, seasoning and egg well together. Make round balls, about 5 cm | 2 inches in diameter. Fry in butter. Remove meatballs and make gravy with butter and flour, add stock. Let meatballs simmer in gravy for 20 minutes. Serves 4.

MOCK HARE Kjøttpudding

250 g | 1/2 lb beef
250 g | 1/2 lb pork, lean
breadcrumbs
1 teaspoon salt
1/4 teaspoon pepper
250 g | 1/2 lb | 1 1/2 cups
prunes
40 cl | 3/4 pint | 2 cups
water
250 g | 1/2 lb | 1 cup
butter
3 tablespoons cream

Wash prunes and leave in water 24 hours. Stew until tender. Remove stones. Pass meat through mincer 4 times. Add breadcrumbs, salt and pepper. Form into thick, oblong loaf, stuff with prunes. Brown in butter, add water or stock. Simmer 1 hour. Remove meat. Bring gravy to brisk boil and add the cream. Serves 6.

CHICKEN A LA MANOR Kylling stekt i gryte

2 spring chickens
3 tablespoons butter
1 teaspoon salt
1 lump sugar
parsley
1/4 l | 3/8 pint | 1 cup
chicken stock
8 tablespoons | 1/2 cup
cream

Clean chickens, dry and stuff with cold butter, 1/2 lump sugar and chopped parsley. Brown in a heavy saucepan, sprinkle with salt, baste with stock. Add butter from time to time. Remove chickens and cut in two. Add cream, butter and 1 tablespoon cold water to gravy. Bring to a brisk boil. Arrange chickens on a hot dish. Garnish with crisply fried parsley. Serves 4.

BACON OMELETTE Baconomelett

4 eggs
2 tablespoons flour
35 cl | 5/8 pint | 1 1/2 cups milk
1/2 teaspoon salt
8 thin rashers bacon
chives

Mix eggs, flour, milk and salt. Set aside for 1 hour. Brown bacon, remove when crisp. Pour off fat, return bacon to pan. Pour egg-mixture over bacon and fry over a low heat. When half done sprinkle with chopped chives. Turn and fry on other side until firm. Cut in wedges and serve from pan. Serves 4.

HAMBURGERS Karbonader

500 g | 1 lb beef
2 mashed potatoes
1/2 teaspoon salt
1/2 teaspoon pepper
1/4 l | 3/8 pint | 1 cup cold water
1 large onion
250 g | 1/2 lb | 1 cup butter

Cube meat and pass through mincer 3 times. Add mashed potatoes and seasoning. Add water gradually and stir until smooth. Make 12 flat cakes. Brown sliced onion in butter. Remove and keep hot. Fry cakes in onion butter until nicely brown. Arrange on hot dish, garnish with fried onions and pour brown butter over. Serves 4.

CHRISTMAS HAM Juleskinke

1 fresh ham (4 to 4 1/2 kg | 9 to 10 lb)
2 bottles light beer
2 bottles dark beer
750 g | 1 1/2 lb | 3 cups coarse salt
250 g | 1/2 lb | 1 cup sugar
1 tablespoon saltpetre

Rub ham with 1 tablespoon sugar, 3 tablespoons fine salt and the saltpetre. Leave 24 hours. Boil beer, sugar, coarse salt and saltpetre together. Cool and pour over ham. Leave in brine 3 weeks. Turn daily. Hang to dry in airy place. Smoke. When ready simmer 4 hours in boiling, unsalted water. Cool in stock. Remove rind. Serve for Christmas cold as a lunch dish or hot with fresh vegetables for dinner. Leave ham in stock to keep juicy.

CURED MUTTON Fenalår

1 leg of mutton
2 tablespoons brandy
1 teaspoon saltpetre
1 kg | 2 lb | 3 cups fine
salt
175 g | 6 oz | 1/2 cup
syrup (molasses)
1/4 l | 3/8 pint | 1 cup
water

Rub meat with brandy. Make a thick brine of all other ingredients and leave the meat in the brine for about a week. Turn several times every day.

Then make a new brine of:
10 l | 2–2 1/2 gallons water
2 kg | 4 lb | 8 cups
coarse salt
500 g | 1 lb | 2 cups
sugar
1 tablespoon saltpetre

Boil all ingredients together and cool. Leave the meat in brine for 6 days. Smoke and hang to dry in an airy place for about 3 months. Serve cut in thin slices with scrambled eggs, creamed spinach or spring vegetables.

PTARMIGAN Stekt rype

4 ptarmigan
250 g | 1/2 lb | 1 cup
butter
1 teaspoon salt
40 cl | 3/4 pint | 2 cups
water
40 cl | 3/4 pint | 2 cups
thick sour cream
2 slices goat's milk cheese
1 tablespoon cold water
1 tablespoon butter

Clean ptarmigan thoroughly and brown with lots of butter in a heavy saucepan. Sprinkle with salt and add boiling water gradually. Baste frequently and add a pat of butter from time to time. Simmer 1 hour, add 1/4 l | 3/8 pint | 1 cup sour cream, and simmer for 45 minutes. Baste frequently. Remove ptarmigan when done, bring gravy to a brisk boil, add remaining cream, cheese and butter. Add cold water to make gravy curdle and a few drops gravy browning, if desired. There should be no speck of flour in a first-class ptarmigan gravy. Cut birds in two, arrange on a hot dish and pour over some gravy. Serve with cranberry relish and browned potatoes. Serve the rest of the gravy in a sauceboat. Serves 6.

40

BEEFBURGERS A LA LINDSTRÖM Biff à la Lindström

500 g | 1 lb beef
1 egg yolk
1 teaspoon salt
½ teaspoon pepper
75 g | 2½ oz | ½ cup
pickled beetroot, diced
3 tablespoons chopped
onion
1 tablespoon capers
3 tablespoons milk

Mince meat, mix the ingredients and work well. Add milk gradually. Form into large flat cakes, fry in margarine to a crisp brown. Serves 4.

STUFFED CAULIFLOWER Fylt blomkål

1 large firm cauliflower
500 g | 1 lb | 2 cups
meat, finely minced
2 tomatoes
parsley

Cover bottom of oblong, well-greased baking dish with 250 g | ½ lb | 1 cup minced meat. Parboil cauliflower for 3 minutes in water with small amount of salt. Cut in small flowerets. Put on top of meat. Add the rest of the meat and steam for 1 hour. Turn out on to a hot serving dish. Decorate with cauliflower flowerets, tomatoes and parsley. Serve with rich, brown gravy or tomato sauce. Serves 4.

"PUSS PASS" (Delicious autumn and winter dish)

1 kg | 2 lb mutton
8 large potatoes
4 large carrots
½ head cabbage, sliced
1 teaspoon black pepper-
corns
1 tablespoon flour
¼ l | ⅜ pint | 1 cup
water

Wash meat and cut in pieces. Place in a heavy saucepan, fat pieces on the bottom, the rest in layers with cabbage. Sprinkle with salt, flour and herbs. Pour water over and simmer tightly covered 3–4 hours. Serves 8.

LIVER PASTE Leverpostei

500 g | 1 lb pork liver *250 g | ¹/₂ lb fresh fat pork* *3 tablespoons butter* *3 tablespoons flour* *8 tablespoons | ¹/₂ cup |* *milk* *1 egg* *1 teaspoon salt* *¹/₂ teaspoon pepper* *1 teaspoon minced onion* *2 anchovies*	Soak liver for 2 hours in cold water containing a little vinegar. Cube and pass 4 or 5 times through mincer together with meat, onion and anchovies. Make thick white sauce, add liver mixture which has been seasoned and blended with beaten egg. Pour mixture into well greased, oblong baking dish, set in a tin of hot water and bake in a moderate oven (Mark 4: 180° C/350° F) for 1 hour. Cool. Turn out. This makes a very nice sandwich spread.

FORCEMEAT BALLS Medisterkaker

250 g | ¹/₂ lb veal *500 g | 1 lb lean pork* *2 teaspoons salt* *1 teaspoon pepper* *1 tablespoon potato flour* *1 tablespoon bread-* *crumbs* *¹/₄ l | ³/₈ pint | 1 cup cold* *boiled milk* *125 g | 4 oz | ¹/₂ cup* *butter*	Dice meat and pass through mincer 3 times. Add flour, crumbs and seasoning. Stir in milk, a little at a time. Form into round balls and brown in butter. Serve with cooked prunes, apple sauce and pickled cabbage. Serves 8.

POUNDED STEAK Bankekjøtt

500 g | 1 lb beef *1 tablespoon salt* *3 tablespoons flour* *3 tablespoons butter* *40 cl | ³/₄ pint | 2 cups* *boiling water* *3 bay leaves*	Cut meat in slices, pound lightly. Coat with a mixture of flour and salt, brown in butter. Season. Place meat in a heavy pan with bay leaves. Add water and simmer tightly covered 1¹/₂ hours. Serves 4. Make gravy by adding water to drippings in pan.

MOCK PTARMIGAN Falsk rype

Proceed exactly as for Beef Olives, (page 34), using venison instead of beef. Stuff with forcemeat and strips of fat pork. Add a few drops of gravy browning and a little goat's milk cheese to the gravy. Serves 4.

SMOKED CURED HAM Spekeskinke

1 large fresh ham (4½ to 5½ kg | 10 to 12 lb)
3 tablespoons salt
3 tablespoons sugar
1 teaspoon saltpetre
10 l | 2 (2½ U.S.) gallons water
1½ kg | 3 lb | 5 cups fine salt
500 g | 1 lb | 1⅓ cups molasses
500 g | 1 lb | 2 cups sugar
125 g | 4 oz saltpetre

Rub ham with salt, sugar and saltpetre. Leave for 3 days. Make a brine of water, sugar, molasses and saltpetre. Boil and cool. Leave ham in brine 7 to 8 weeks. Hang to dry 48 hours. Smoke. Hang in an airy place 3 months.

SADDLE OF VENISON Dyresadel

2 kg | 4 lb saddle of venison
1 tablespoon salt
1 teaspoon pepper
125 g | 4 oz | ½ cup butter
1 tablespoon margarine
1 tablespoon flour
40 cl | ¾ pint | 2 cups boiling water
¼ l | ⅜ pint | 1 cup thick sour cream
1 slice goat's milk cheese
1 tablespoon butter

Wash and dry meat, spread with cold butter and season. Put into a very hot oven (Mark 8: 230° C/450° F). When nicely browned, add water and baste frequently. Roast for 2½ to 3 hours. Make brown gravy from margarine and flour, gradually add the pan juices. Boil briskly for 5 minutes, add cream and cheese. Bring to the boil once more, add 1 tablespoon cold water and 1 tablespoon chilled butter. Serves 8.

ESCALOPES OF VEAL Wienerschnitzel

500 g | 1 lb veal
1 egg white
8 tablespoons | ½ cup
breadcrumbs
3 tablespoons butter
1 teaspoon salt
½ teaspoon pepper
4 slices lemon
4 fillets of anchovies
2 tablespoons capers
8 tablespoons | ½ cup
boiling water

Cut meat in 4 slices. Flatten with mallet. Coat each piece of meat with egg white and crumbs. Fry until nicely browned and very tender. Make the gravy by adding water to the juices in the pan. Serve garnished with lemon slices, anchovies and capers. Serves 4.

SKIPPER'S STEW Skipperns gryte

500 g | 1 lb veal
4 large potatoes
¼ l | ⅜ pint | 1 cup boiling water
salt, pepper
1 tablespoon chopped parsley
4 pats butter

Cut the meat and potatoes into cubes. Cook for one hour in water, add salt and pepper. When serving sprinkle with chopped parsley and dot with butter. Serves 4.

VENISON HAMBURGERS Dyrekarbonader

500 g | 1 lb venison
4 slices lean salt pork
1 egg
8 tablespoons | ½ cup
meat stock
8 tablespoons | ½ cup
sour cream
3 tablespoons butter
1 teaspoon salt
¼ teaspoon pepper
3 slices goat's milk cheese
1 tablespoon cold water

Pass meat and pork through the mincer 3 times. Add lightly beaten egg, salt and pepper. Stir in the stock. Form into large cakes and brown in butter. Make gravy by adding cream and cheese to the pan juices. Bring to a brisk boil and add cold water to make the gravy curdle. Serves 4.

44

CRUMBED BREAST OF VEAL Panert kalvebryst

1 kg | 2 lb breast of veal
90 cl | 1½ pints | 4 cups
water
1 tablespoon salt
1 egg white
8 tablespoons | ½ cup
breadcrumbs
1 teaspoon salt
¼ teaspoon pepper
2 tablespoons butter
¼ l | ⅜ pint | 1 cup meat
stock

Wash meat and cut in pieces. Put into boiling water with very little salt. Bring to the boil. Skim carefully. Simmer 1½ hours. Remove meat, dry and coat with mixture of egg white and crumbs. Fry to a crisp brown in butter. Sprinkle with salt and pepper. Add stock to frying pan and use for gravy. Serve with green peas and fried potatoes. Pour the gravy into a sauceboat. Serves 6.

Vegetables and Salads

Vegetables, rich in vitamins and mineral salts, health-giving and easily pre-
pared, form an important part of the Norwegian diet. The housewife knows how
to serve them either as a main dish or as an accompaniment to fish or meat.
Fresh green salad appears on the dinner-table all through the summer. The
Norwegian housewife has learnt from her French sister how to make a good
salad dressing — she is lavish with the oil and niggardly with the vinegar.

But alas! — lettuces are costly in winter, and Norwegians must often replace
them with a variety of raw vegetable salads, which provide the extra vitamins
they need to maintain their health through the long, dark winter.

CUCUMBER SALAD Agurksalat

1 large fresh cucumber
2 tablespoons boiling
water
1/4 teaspoon salt
3 tablespoons sugar
1/2 teaspoon pepper
1/4 l | 3/8 pint | 1 cup
vinegar
parsley

Mix water, salt, pepper and sugar. Bring to the boil. Cool, add vinegar. Clean, but do not peel cucumber, slice very thinly. Pour dressing over and allow to stand for 15 minutes. Sprinkle with chopped parsley. This makes a crisp, crunchy salad. No vitamins lost in the process. Serves 6.

NORWEGIAN LETTUCE SALAD Bladsalat

2 heads of lettuce
8 tablespoons | 1/2 cup
thick sour cream
2 teaspoons vinegar
1 teaspoon sugar
1/4 teaspoon mustard
1 hard-boiled egg

Clean lettuce thoroughly and strain off all water. Crisp in the refrigerator. Whip cream with sugar. Add seasoning and blend with lettuce. Garnish with wedges of egg. Serves 4.

ASPARAGUS A LA SKAUGUM Asparges à la Skaugum

500 g | 1 lb fresh aspara-
gus
1 tablespoon margarine
1 tablespoon flour
1/4 l | 3/8 pint | 1 cup
asparagus stock
2 egg yolks
1 hard-boiled egg,
chopped
chopped parsley

Cook asparagus for 15–20 minutes in water with small amount of salt. Make a thick white sauce, add egg yolks. Arrange hot asparagus on a serving dish, cover with a little sauce, sprinkle with parsley and chopped egg. Serve the rest of the sauce in a sauceboat. Serves 4.

ADMIRAL'S CAULIFLOWER Admiralens blomkål

1 large head cauliflower
75 g | 2 1/2 oz | 1/2 cup
peeled prawns
8 tablespoons | 1/2 cup
mayonnaise
3 drops green colouring
2 hard-boiled eggs
2 tomatoes
parsley

Clean cauliflower and cook in water with very little salt for about 20 minutes. Strain and cool. Place on a round serving dish, cover with mayonnaise coloured light green. Sprinkle with prawns. Garnish with sliced eggs and tomatoes. Place a large sprig of parsley on top of the admiral's hat. Serves 4.

SUMMER SALAD Sommersalat

1 head lettuce
2 tomatoes
2 boiled potatoes
90 g | 3 oz | 1/2 cup
cooked green peas
1 hard-boiled egg,
chopped
4 tablespoons oil
2 tablespoons vinegar
1 tablespoon mustard
1 teaspoon salt
1 teaspoon sugar
pinch pepper

Slice potatoes, eggs and lettuce. Blend dressing and pour over vegetables. Garnish with sliced tomatoes. Serves 4.

CAULIFLOWER Aunt Tilla's recipe – Blomkål

1 large cauliflower
3 tablespoons browned
butter
2 tablespoons finely chopped parsley
3 tablespoons bread-
·crumbs
1 hard-boiled egg, chop-
ped

Clean cauliflower. Leave 1 hour in salt water. Cook for 20 minutes. Brown butter in frying pan, add egg, breadcrumbs and parsley. Cook until thick. Pour over (hot) cauliflower. Serves 4.

MOCK MUSHROOMS Falsk sopp

2 tomatoes
4 eggs
400 g | 14 oz | 2 cups
cooked, chopped spinach
2 tablespoons butter
8 tablespoons | 1/2 cup
cream
1/4 teaspoon sugar
1/2 teaspoon salt
2 tablespoons flour

Make a thick sauce of butter, flour and cream. Add sugar, salt and spi-nach. Keep hot. Boil eggs for 8 mi-nutes, put immediately into cold water and peel. Cut off tops to make them stand firmly. Place eggs in hot spinach, place one half scooped to-mato on top of each egg, sprinkle with chopped egg whites. Serves 4.

NORWEGIAN HERRING SALAD Sildesalat

2 salted herrings
2 boiled potatoes
2 apples
1 small pickled cucumber
4 slices pickled beetroots
1 tablespoon chopped
onion   ·
1/4 l | 3/8 pint | 1 cup thick
sour cream
1 tablespoon sugar
2 tablespoons vinegar

Clean herrings and soak in water 12 hours. Dice herrings, potatoes, cu-cumber, apples and beetroot. Whip cream with sugar, season. Mix all ingredients and set aside for 1 hour in a cool place. Put into bowl, decor-ate with wedges of hard-boiled egg, finely chopped beetroot and chop-ped parsley. Serves 6.

POTATO SALAD (cold) Potetsalat, kald

8 boiled firm potatoes	Slice potatoes. Mix all other ingredients and pour over. Leave 2 hours. Sprinkle with finely chopped chives. Serves 4.
3 tablespoons oil	
1 tablespoon vinegar	
1 teaspoon sugar	
1/4 teaspoon pepper	
chives	

POTATO SALAD (hot) Potetsalat, varm

8 boiled firm potatoes	Peel and slice potatoes. Fry onion in margarine until golden brown. Mix vinegar and water, add seasoning and onion. Allow to simmer for about 5 minutes. Heat potatoes carefully in hot dressing. Serves 4.
3 tablespoons margarine	
8 tablespoons | 1/2 cup water	
1 chopped onion	
2 tablespoons sugar	
1/4 teaspoon pepper	
3 tablespoons vinegar	

EGGS BAKED IN TOMATOES Bakte tomater med egg

4 even-sized tomatoes	Grease dishes, put one scooped tomato into each dish. Pour one raw egg carefully into each tomato. Bake in a moderately hot oven (Mark 4: 180° C/350° F) for 10–12 minutes. Serve immediately. Serves 4.
4 eggs	
2 tablespoons butter	
4 small baking dishes	

FRIED TOMATOES AND EGG Stekte tomater og egg

4 large tomatoes	Slice tomatoes, fry in butter together with onion. Add water and seasoning. Allow to simmer for 5 minutes. Pour eggs over carefully and fry until the whites are firm and the yolks soft. Serves 4.
1 chopped onion	
2 tablespoons butter	
salt	
pepper	
1 tablespoon water	
4 eggs	

50

RAW VEGETABLE SALAD I Råkostsalat I

40 g | 1¹/2 oz | ¹/2 cup
cabbage, shredded
¹/2 root of celeriac, grated
2 raw apples, diced
¹/4 l | ³/8 pint | 1 cup
mayonnaise
1 teaspoon lemon juice
1 teaspoon parsley
1 teaspoon sugar

Flavour mayonnaise with sugar and lemon juice. Blend with apples and vegetables. Sprinkle with parsley. Serves 4.

RAW VEGETABLE SALAD II Råkostsalat II

1 head lettuce
1 cucumber
2 tomatoes
¹/2 cauliflower
8 tablespoons | ¹/2 cup
mayonnaise
dill

Clean and dice vegetables. Blend with mayonnaise and sprinkle with finely chopped dill. Serves 4.

RAW VEGETABLE SALAD III Råkostsalat III

1 cauliflower, snow-white
160 g | 5¹/2 oz | 1 cup
raisins
8 tablespoons | ¹/2 cup
mayonnaise

Clean and chop cauliflower. Blend with raisins and mayonnaise. Serves 4.

Desserts, Puddings and Sweets

BROWN BETTY Tilslørte bondepiker

*1 kg | 2 lb cooking apples
175 to 250 g | 6 to 8
oz | 3/4 to 1 cup sugar
90 g | 3 oz | 6 table-
spoons butter
1/4 l | 3/8 pint | 1 cup
double cream
250 g | 8 oz | 6 cups soft
brown breadcrumbs (pre-
ferably from dark rye
bread)
90 g | 3 oz | 4 table-
spoons grated chocolate*

Peel apples, slice and cook to consistency of apple sauce in 1 tablespoon water. Sweeten with 125 to 175 g | 4 to 6 oz | 1 1/2 to 3/4 cup of sugar, according to taste. Cool. Fry crumbs in butter until brown and crisp, stirring in 4 tablespoons sugar towards the end of frying. Cool. Arrange apple sauce and crumbs in layers in a serving dish. Decorate with whipped cream and sprinkle with grated chocolate. Serves 6.

APPLE DUMPLINGS Epler i slåbrok

*250 g | 1/2 lb | 2 cups flour
150 g | 5 oz | 2/3 cup mar-
garine
1/2 teaspoon salt
4 tablespoons cold water
8 cooking apples
125 g | 4 oz | 1/2 cup
sugar
1 egg white, stiffly beaten
1 tablespoon ground blan-
ched almonds*

Mix flour, salt and margarine to the consistency of fine breadcrumbs. Add water and roll out the pastry very thinly. Cut into 8 square pieces. Wash and core apples, and fill each opening with sugar. Place each apple on a piece of pastry, fold around apple. Coat with stiff egg white and sprinkle with almonds. Place on greased baking sheet and bake for 25 minutes in a moderate oven (Mark 5: 190° C/ 375° F). Serve lukewarm with whipped cream or custard sauce. Serves 4.

APPLE MERINGUE Eplemarengs

6 apples
8 tablespoons | ¹/₂ cup
water
250 g | 4 oz | ¹/₂ cup
sugar
vanilla essence
4 egg whites
4 teaspoons cider vinegar
135 g | 4¹/₂ oz | 1 cup
icing sugar
3 tablespoons almonds,
chopped

Peel apples and boil in sugar syrup to the consistency of apple sauce. Pour into a baking dish. Beat egg whites very stiffly, add vinegar and sugar, beat for another 5 minutes. Pour meringue mixture over the apple sauce, sprinkle with almonds and bake in a slow oven (Mark ¹/₂: 140° C/275° F) for 35 to 40 minutes. Serves 6.

BLUEBERRY CAKE Blåbærkake

320 g | 10¹/₂ oz | 2 cups
blueberries
60 g | 2 oz | 2 cups
breadcrumbs
250 g | ¹/₂ lb | 1 cup
sugar
125 g | 4 oz | ¹/₂ cup
butter
8 tablespoons | ¹/₂ cup
double cream

Grease a baking dish. Arrange berries, crumbs and sugar in layers, crumbs on top. Pour melted butter over and bake in a moderate oven (Mark 5: 190° C/375° F) 1 hour. Serve lukewarm with a bowl of whipped cream. Serves 4.

BLUEBERRY PANCAKES Blåbærpannekaker

125 g | 4 oz | 1 cup flour
4 tablespoons sugar
¹/₂ teaspoon salt
¹/₄ l | ³/₈ pint | 1 cup milk
2 eggs

Take 350 g | ³/₄ lb | 1 cup blueberry jam or fresh berries stirred with sugar until sugar dissolves. Make batter and set it aside for 1 hour. Add berries. Fry one thick pancake. Serve on hot round dish. Cut in wedges, sprinkle with sugar. Or: Fry thin pancakes, arrange in layers with berries. Serve hot. Serves 4.

CRÈME CARAMEL Karamellpudding

250 g | ½ lb | 1 cup
sugar
8 tablespoons | ½ cup
boiling water
40 cl | ¾ pint | 2 cups
milk
4 eggs
2 tablespoons sugar
vanilla essence

Caramelize sugar over a moderate heat. Add water and let it simmer for about 5 minutes until smooth. Pour immediately into mould, cover bottom and sides. Whip eggs with sugar, add milk and cream, boiling hot. Cool for about 5 minutes. Pour into mould and steam 70 to 75 minutes in a pan of hot water. Let it cool completely before turning out. Decorate with whipped cream. Serves 8.

COURT DESSERT Hoffdessert

20 small meringues
40 cl | ¾ pint | 2 cups
double cream
1 tablespoon sugar
125 g | 4 oz | 4 squares
unsweetened chocolate
8 tablespoons | ½ cup
strong coffee
1 tablespoon blanched almonds, chopped

Dissolve chocolate in coffee and stir until smooth. Place 10 meringues in a dish, pour over half of the chocolate mixture, add the rest of the meringues. Decorate with whipped cream. Pour the rest of the chocolate mixture over to form a pattern. Sprinkle with almonds. Serves 8.

CREAM DOTS Fløtelapper

40 cl | ¾ pint | 2 cups
thick sour cream
2 tablespoons flour
2 tablespoons rice flour or
cornflour
2 eggs
1 tablespoon sugar
1½ teaspoons ground
cardamom
2 tablespoons butter
jam

Mix cream, flour, rice flour, eggs, sugar and cardamom. Beat to a smooth batter. Stand aside for 1 hour. Drop batter with a spoon in dots on to a hot frying pan greased with butter. Cook over a low heat until light brown on both sides. Serve with sugar and jam. Serves 4.

CREAM OF RICE Riskrem

40 cl | 3/4 pint | 2 cups
rice porridge
1/4 l | 3/8 pint | 1 cup
double cream
1 tablespoon sugar
1 tablespoon blanched
almonds, chopped
jam

Whip cream with sugar, blend with porridge, add almonds and serve with jam or fruit sauce. Serves 4.

GRANDMOTHER'S DESSERT Bestemorsdessert

60 g | 2 oz | 2 cups dark
breadcrumbs, soft
4 tablespoons jam
2 tablespoons margarine
2 tablespoons sugar
8 tablespoons | 1/2 cup
double cream

Caramelize sugar and margarine. Add breadcrumbs. Cool. Stir in the jam just before serving. Serve in 4 individual dishes. Decorate with whipped cream. Serves 4.

MARCH SNOW Marssnø

40 cl | 3/4 pint | 2 cups
double cream
1 tablespoon (1 envelope)
gelatine powder
3 tablespoons sugar
juice of 1 lemon
peel of 1 lemon

Dissolve gelatine. Whip cream with sugar, add lemon juice, peel and gelatine. Mix well. Pour into serving dish. Cool. Serve with fruit juice or strawberry jam. Serves 6.

MAGIC CREAM Trollkrem

3 egg whites
3 tablespoons sugar
juice of 1/2 lemon
350 g | 3/4 lb | 1 cup
apple sauce or
red whortleberry jam

Beat egg whites until very stiff, add lemon juice and sugar. Whip to a fluffy cream. The more you whip the more the cream increases in volume, hence the name magic cream. Add apple sauce, or red whortleberry jam if you want a pink cream. Serves 6.

56

GREAT-GRANDMOTHER'S DESSERT Oldemorsdessert

2 tablespoons fine castor
sugar
1 kg | 2¼ lb | 3 cups
apple or plum jam
¼ l | ⅜ pint | 1 cup
double cream
4 tablespoons sugar
4 eggs
3 tablespoons finely chopped almonds

Cover the bottom of a large baking dish with jam. Beat eggs and sugar to a thick cream. Pour over the jam. Sprinkle with almonds and cover with stiffly beaten egg whites. Bake in a moderate oven (Mark 4: 180° C/ 350° F) for 30 minutes. Serve luke-warm with chilled whipped cream in a separate bowl. Serves 6.

WHITE LADY Hvite dame

4 eggs
2 tablespoons sugar
1 tablespoon (1 envelope)
gelatine powder
35 cl | ⅝ pint | 1½ cups
double cream
60 g | 2 oz | ⅔ cup
ground almonds
350 g | ¾ lb | 1 cup jam

Whip egg yolks with sugar. Add ground almonds and jam. Whip cream and egg whites separately. Mix all ingredients together. Add dissol-ved gelatine. Pour into a moist mould. Chill 3 hours. Turn out on to a chilled serving dish. Serve with fruit sauce. Serves 6.

MONKS Munker

3 eggs
2 tablespoons sugar
40 cl | ¾ pint | 2 cups
thick sour milk
1 tablespoon butter
2 teaspoons baking
powder
300 g | 10 oz | 2½ cups
flour
3 teaspoons ground
cardamom
1½ teaspoons ground
cinnamon

Whisk the eggs and sugar together, add all other ingredients, spices last. Heat special scooped iron, pour one tablespoon of batter into each hole. Turn often to prevent burning before monks are done. Serve hot with jam and sprinkled with icing sugar. Ser-ves 8.

PANCAKES Pannekaker

4 eggs
125 g | 4 oz | 1 cup flour
1/4 l | 3/8 pint | 1 cup milk
pinch salt
1 tablespoon sugar
1 tablespoon butter

Beat eggs and sugar together, add all other ingredients. Let the batter stand for 1 hour. Melt butter in a frying pan, pour in batter with a spoon and cook very thin pancakes. Serve with sugar and strawberry jam. Serves 6.

POOR KNIGHTS Arme Riddere

8 slices stale white bread
60 cl | 1 pint | 2 1/2 cups milk
1 egg
1 tablespoon sugar
1 teaspoon ground cinnamon
2 tablespoons margarine

Beat egg yolk with milk, remove crust and soak bread in egg and milk mixture for 15 minutes. Sprinkle with sugar and cinnamon. Fry until light brown in margarine. Serve hot with jam or jelly. Serves 4.

THRIFTY CREAM DESSERT Hverdagskrem

3/4 l | 1 1/4 pints | 3 cups sour milk
1/4 l | 3/8 pint | 1 cup double cream
30 g | 1 oz | 1 cup breadcrumbs
1 tablespoon sugar
175 g | 6 oz | 1/2 cup jam

Whip cream, milk and sugar until thick. Add crumbs. Sprinkle with sugar and serve with jam. Serves 4.

CLOUDBERRY CAKE Multekake

4 slices plain sponge or Madeira cake
2 egg whites
175 g | 6 oz | 1 cup cloudberries
2 tablespoons sugar

Cover each piece of cake with cloudberries. Whip whites stiffly, add sugar, whip once more, spread meringue over cakes and bake in a very slow oven (Mark 1/4: 120° C/225° F) for 6 to 8 minutes. Serves 4.

58

JUNE DESSERT Junidessert

500 g | 1 lb | 5¹/₃ cups
ground almonds
500 g | 1 lb | 2¹/₃ cups
castor sugar
3 egg whites
500 g | 1 lb | 5 cups rhu-
barb, cubed
125 g | 4 oz | ¹/₂ cup
sugar
3 tablespoons water
4 bananas
8 tablespoons | ¹/₂ cup
double cream

Stir almonds, the castor sugar and egg whites until smooth. Pour into well greased round baking dish. Bake in slow oven (Mark ¹/₄: 130° C/250° F) for 45 minutes. Cool. Gently stew the rhubarb with the sugar and water in the oven or in a heavy pan. Cover cake with stewed rhubarb. Decorate with banana slices and whipped cream. Serves 8.

RED JELLY Rødgrøt

³/₄ l | 1¹/₄ pints | 3 cups
water
¹/₄ l | ³/₈ pint | 1 cup red-
currant juice
¹/₄ l | ³/₈ pint | 1 cup
raspberry juice
3 tablespoons potato flour
vanilla essence
10 blanched almonds,
chopped

Bring juice and water to the boil. Make a thin paste of flour and cold water, add to hot juice. Stir vigorously. Remove from heat. Add vanilla. Pour into a serving dish, sprinkle with sugar and almonds. Serve cold with milk or cream. Serves 4.

SNOW MOUSSE (For special guests) Snøkrem

90 cl | 1¹/₂ pints | 1 quart
ice-cream
8 small macaroons
3 tablespoons cherry jam
3 tablespoons blanched
almonds, chopped
60 g | 2 oz | ¹/₂ cup
chopped walnuts
4 sliced figs
10 dates, sliced
1 glass sherry

When ice-cream starts to thicken, add macaroons, jam, almonds, walnuts, fruit and wine. Pour back into freezer tray and freeze until ready. Turn out on to a chilled serving dish. Decorate with slices of pineapple, walnuts, cocktail cherries and frozen whipped cream. Serve with wafers. Serves 10.

STEWED RHUBARB Rabarbrakompott

500 g | 1 lb | 5 cups
fresh rhubarb
90 cl | 1½ pints | 4 cups
water
125 g | 4 oz | ½ cup
sugar
1½ teaspoons potato flour

Clean rhubarb, cut into pieces. Simmer with water and sugar until tender. Make a paste of flour and 1 tablespoon cold water. Bring rhubarb to a brisk boil, remove from heat, add paste immediately and stir vigorously. Cool. Sprinkle with sugar and serve with milk or cream.

IRRESISTIBLE DESSERT "Jeg kan ikke la være"

4 eggs, separated
125 g | 4 oz | ½ cup
sugar
juice of ½ lemon
1 tablespoon (1 envelope)
gelatine powder

Whip egg yolks with sugar until foamy. Add the stiffly beaten egg whites, dissolved gelatine and lemon juice. Mix well. Pour into a serving dish and allow to stand until firm (about 4 hours). Decorate with whipped cream, cherries and macaroons. Serves 4.

RUM PUDDING Rompudding

¾ l | 1¼ pints | 3 cups
cream
2 tablespoons sugar
1½ tablespoons (1½ envelopes) gelatine powder
2 eggs
6 tablespoons rum

Bring cream to the boil, add sugar and dissolved gelatine. Whip egg yolks with the sugar until foamy. Mix with cream and stir until cool. Add rum and the stiffly beaten egg whites. Pour into a serving dish. Chill for 2 hours. Serve with strawberry jam and biscuits. Serves 6.

LITTLE MISS MUFFETS Melkeringer

1½ l | 2½ pints | 6 cups
milk, lukewarm
6 tablespoons | ⅓ cup
thick sour cream
sugar and breadcrumbs

Pour 1 tablespoon sour cream into a deep dish or soup plate. Pour milk over, place in warm, airy place for about 24 hours until the milk thickens. Cool. Sprinkle with sugar and crumbs. Serves 4.

60

Bread and Cakes

Cleanliness is the first rule in baking, and next comes accuracy: measure and weigh carefully, never make a wild guess. Finally, remember to use good-quality, fresh ingredients. If you observe these three golden rules, your baking is bound to be a success.

It's well worth baking bread and cakes at home, it's fun, and there is no pleasure equal to the housewife's pride when her handiwork is successful.

FRENCH BREAD Franskbrød

500 g | 1 lb | 4 cups plain flour
1 teaspoon salt
1 1/2 tablespoons butter
15 g | 1/2 oz yeast or 1 1/2 teaspoons dried yeast (or 1/2 yeast cake)
40 cl | 3/4 pint | 2 cups tepid milk

Mix flour, salt and yeast, add milk and work into a fairly soft dough. Allow to rise 1 hour, shape into two oblong loaves, place in well-greased tins and allow to rise for another 30 minutes. Brush with egg and bake in a hot oven (Mark 6: 200° C/400° F) for 30 minutes. Makes 2 loaves.

CRISPBREAD Knekkebrød

350 g | 3/4 lb | 3 cups plain flour
250 g | 1/2 lb | 2 cups rye flour
60 g | 2 oz | 1/4 cup butter
1 tablespoon sugar
1 teaspoon baking powder
1/4 l | 3/8 pint | 1 cup water

Knead flour, baking powder and butter and add water. Work dough well, roll out thinly and cut into oblong pieces. Bake until crisp in a slow oven (Mark 2: 150° C/300° F), cool and separate. Makes 60.

ISSANTS Horn

³/₈ pint | 1 cup tepid	Mix yeast with some of the milk. Blend the rest of the milk with the butter, beat the egg and add to the flour and yeast. Knead dough and allow to rise for 30 minutes. Divide the dough into quarters. Roll out thinly into four circles, cut in quarters and roll up into croissants. Allow to rise for 25 minutes, brush with melted butter and bake for 15 minutes in a hot oven (Mark 6: 200° C/400° F). Makes 16.
| 4 oz | ½ cup	
1 lb | 4 cups flour	
poon sugar	
oz fresh yeast or	
poon dried yeast	
t cake)	

MOMENTS Pleskener

rated	Whisk yolks of egg with sugar, add flour and stiffly beaten whites of egg. Spoon dough with a teaspoon on to a greased baking sheet, spacing well apart, as the biscuits are liable to run. Bake until pale brown in a moderate oven (Mark 3: 170° C/325° F). Makes 40.
| 1 cup cas-	
1 cup flour	

SEN'S BISCUITS Mor Monsen

cup	Melt butter and stir in sugar. Add the eggs one at a time, and then the flour and vanilla sugar. Put the dough on to baking sheets lined with greased greaseproof paper and sprinkle with finely chopped blanched almonds and currants. Bake until golden brown in a moderately hot oven (Mark 5: 190° C/375° F). Cut to appropriate shapes with a sharp knife. Makes 30 biscuits.
p cas-	
ps	

ROLLS Rundstykker

500 g | 1 lb | 4 cups flour 2 tablespoons cold margarine ½ teaspoon salt 1 egg 1 teaspoon sugar 20 g | ¾ oz fresh yeast or 1 tablespoon dried yeast (or 1 yeast cake) 35 cl | ⁵/₈ pint | 1½ cups milk	Cream the yeast with a little of the milk. Rub the margarine into the flour, salt and sugar. Add the egg, yeast mixture and the tepid milk. Knead well. Shape into rolls and allow to rise for 30 minutes. Brush with egg and bake in a moderate oven (Mark 5: 190° C/375° F) for 15 minutes. Makes 12.

CUSTARD TARTLETS Linser

300 g | 10 oz | 2½ cups flour 250 g | ½ lb | 1 cup butter 4 tablespoons sugar ¼ l | ³/₈ pint | 1 cup thick vanilla custard 2 yolks of egg	Mix flour, butter, sugar and egg yolks and set aside for two hours. Roll out the dough ½ cm | ¼ inch thick and press into small, well-greased patty tins. Place one tablespoon vanilla custard in each tin. Roll out the rest of the dough and make little lids to cover each tartlet. Bake 20 minutes in a moderately hot oven (Mark 4: 180° C/350° F). Makes 16.

MADAME PETERSEN'S POUND CAKE Fru Pedersens pundkake (100-year-old family recipe)

500 g | 1 lb | 4 cups flour 500 g | 1 lb | 2 cups sugar 500 g | 1 lb | 2 cups unsalted butter 500 g | 1 lb eggs (8 standard eggs) 250 g | ½ lb | 1½ cups currants	Cream the unsalted butter with the sugar until white. Beat in the egg yolks, one at a time. Rinse currants, dry and mix with flour and add to mixture. Add stiffly whipped whites of egg. Pour the dough into a well-greased and floured oblong tin, and bake in a moderately hot oven (Mark 3: 170° C/325° F) for 60 minutes. Makes 2 cakes.

WHOLEMEAL BREAD Grahambrød

500 g | 1 lb | 4 cups rye flour
500 g | 1 lb | 4 cups wholewheat flour
40 cl | 3/4 pint | 2 cups water
1/4 l | 3/8 pint | 1 cup milk
350 g | 3/4 lb | 1 cup syrup
20 g | 3/4 oz fresh yeast or 1 tablespoon dried yeast (or 1 yeast cake)
1/2 teaspoon salt

Mix the flour and salt. Cream the yeast with some of the milk. Warm the water, milk and syrup and add to the rest of the ingredients. Knead well. Let dough rise to double size, shape into two oblong loaves and allow to rise for another 30 minutes. Brush with water and bake 45 minutes in a hot oven (Mark 6: 200° C/ 400° F). Makes 2 loaves.

WHITE BREAD Hvetebrød

35 cl | 5/8 pint | 1 1/2 cups tepid milk
20 g | 3/4 oz fresh yeast or 1 tablespoon dried yeast (or 1 yeast cake)
1 tablespoon sugar
1 teaspoon salt
600 g | 1 1/4 lb | 5 cups plain flour

Cream the yeast with some of the milk. Mix the other ingredients, knead the dough and let it rise for one hour. Divide into two and roll into long even "sausages". Place on baking board and allow to rise for 15 minutes. Gash at regular intervals, brush with cold water and place in a hot oven (Mark 8: 230° C/450° F) for 10 minutes. Reduce temperature to Mark 4: 180° C/350° F, and bake for another 15–20 minutes. Makes 2 loaves.

CHEESE BISCUITS Ostekjeks

125 g | 4 oz | 1 cup flour
125 g | 4 oz | 1 cup grated cheese
250 g | 1/2 lb | 1 cup butter
2 yolks of egg

Knead butter, flour and cheese, add eggs to bind the dough. Set aside for one hour. Roll out 1 cm | 1/2 inch thick, cut into circles with an inverted beer glass. Prick discs and bake 6–7 minutes in a moderate oven (Mark 4: 180° C/350° F). Eat freshly baked whilst crisp. Makes 40.

64

BERLIN GARLANDS Berlinerkranser

4 eggs
275 g | 9 oz | 2 cups icing sugar
250 g | 1/2 lb | 2 cups flour
500 g | 1 lb | 2 cups un- salted dairy butter

Stir two hard-
two raw yolk
sugar. Knead
dough altern
in a cool s
and shape
ped white
sugar, a
Bake pa
(Mark 5

OATMEAL BISCUITS Havrekjeks

325 g | 11 oz | 4 cups oatmeal
40 cl | 3/4 pint | 2 cups milk
500 g | 1 lb | 2 cups butter
1 teaspoon vanilla sugar
250 g | 1/2 lb | 2 cups plain flour
2 teaspoons hartshorn

So
C
s

ARISTOCRATS Ar

250 g | 1/2 lb | 2
flour
250 g | 1/2 lb | 1
butter
125 g | 4 oz |
sugar
75 g | 2 oz
chopped bl
monds
1 egg
1/4 teaspo

66

CRO

1/4 l
milk
125 g
butter
500 g
1 table
1 egg
25 g | 1
1 tablesp
(or 1 yea

MELTING

3 eggs, sepa
200 g | 7 oz
tor sugar
125 g | 4 oz

MOTHER MON

250 g | 1/2 lb | 1
butter
200 g | 7 oz | 1 c
tor sugar
250 g | 1/2 lb | 2 cu
flour
4 eggs
75 g | 2 1/2 oz | 1/2
almonds
35 g | 1 1/4 oz | 1/4 cu
currants
1 teaspoon vanilla sug

CHRISTMAS CAKE Julekake

40 cl | ³/₄ pint | 2 cups
lukewarm milk
250 g | ¹/₂ lb | 1 cup
sugar
250 g | ¹/₂ lb | 1 cup melted butter
20 g | ³/₄ oz fresh yeast or
1 tablespoon dried yeast
(or 1 yeast cake)
600 g | 1¹/₄ lb | 5 cups
flour
1 teaspoon ground cardamom
125 g | 4 oz | ³/₄ cup raisins
90 g | 3 oz | ¹/₂ cup
chopped candied peel

Cream the yeast with some of the milk. Dissolve the sugar in the milk and melted butter. Add, with the yeast, to the flour, cardamom, raisins and peel. Knead the dough quickly and allow to rise for 20 minutes. Knead again, shape into two round cakes. Allow to rise for 30 minutes. Brush with egg, bake in a hot oven (Mark 6: 200° C/400° F) for 35–40 minutes. Makes 2 cakes.

SYRUP CAKE Krydderkake (Mock honey cake)

500 g | 1 lb | 1¹/₃ cups
syrup
250 g | ¹/₂ lb | 1 cup margarine
750 g | 1¹/₂ lb | 3 cups
granulated sugar
3 eggs
juice and grated rind of
one lemon
2 teaspoons ground ginger
2 teaspoons ground cardamom
1 kg | 2 lb | 8 cups flour
3 heaped teaspoons baking powder
250 g | ¹/₂ lb | 1 cup
orange marmalade
1 large piece grated candied lemon peel

Heat the syrup, butter and sugar in a large, heavy pan and allow to cool. Beat the eggs lightly, add spices, marmalade, candied peel, flour and baking powder. Fold the second mixture into the cooled syrup. Place the batter in two large well-greased tins and bake for 1 hour in a moderate oven (Mark 5: 190° C/375° F). Makes 2 cakes.

CORNETS Krumkaker

250 g | ½ lb | 1 cup
butter
250 g | ½ lb | 1 cup
sugar
250 g | ½ lb | 2 cups
flour
2 eggs
8 tablespoons | ½ cup
water
2 eggs
1 teaspoon grated lemon
rind

Whisk egg yolks with sugar. Add water and flour. Melt butter, cool, and add lemon rind and stiffly beaten whites of egg. Bake cornets in a greased, patterned, *krumkake* iron, then shape into cornets immediately. Makes 30 cornets.

DOUGHNUTS Berlinerboller

3 tablespoons melted
butter
¼ l | ⅜ pint | 1 cup milk
250 g | ½ lb | 1 cup
sugar
400 g | 14 oz | 3½ cups
flour
4 teaspoons baking
powder
½ teaspoon ground car-
damom
½ teaspoon salt
1 egg
1 yolk of egg

Melt the butter in the milk over a low heat, then cool. Add the sugar, flour, baking powder, spice, salt and eggs, and work into a dough. Set the dough aside for an hour. Roll it out ½ cm | ¼ inch thick and cut with a doughnut cutter. Fry in lard at a temperature of 190° C/370° F. Makes 4 dozen.

GUDNY'S BISCUITS Gudnys kaker

500 g | 1 lb | 4 cups flour
350 g | ¾ lb | 1½ cups
butter
175 g | 6 oz | ¾ cup
sugar
1 teaspoon vanilla sugar

Knead dough, work into a firm «sausage». Cut with a sharp knife into slices about 1 cm | ⅓ inch thick. Bake in a moderate oven (Mark 4: 180° C/350° F) for 15 minutes. Makes 40 biscuits.

KING HAAKON'S CAKE Kong Haakons kake

250 g | ½ lb | 1 cup
butter
200 g | 7 oz | 1 cup cas-
tor sugar
4 eggs, separated
125 g | 4 oz | 1 cup flour
150 g | 5 oz | 1 cup pot-
ato flour
1 teaspoon baking powder
Cream:
3 yolks of egg
3 tablespoons sugar
2 tablespoons cocoa
60 g | 2 oz | 2 squares
chocolate
2 teaspoons flour
¼ l | ⅜ pint | 1 cup
cream

Stir together sugar and butter, add egg yolks, flour sifted with baking powder, and stiffly beaten whites of egg. Bake dough in a greased floured round tin in a moderate oven (Mark 4: 180° C/350° F) for 25 minutes. Cool. Divide cake into three, fill with cream filling as follows:
– Whip egg yolks with sugar, add cocoa and melted chocolate. Mix in flour, bring to boil, cool, and add three tablespoonfuls whipped cream. Cover the cake with marzipan, put King Haakon's initials on top (see picture) and decorate with small Norwegian flags. Serves 10.

TELEGRAPH CAKE Telegrafkake

350 g | ¾ lb | 3 cups
flour
2 teaspoons baking
powder
500 g | 1 lb | 2 cups
sugar
250 g | ½ lb | 1 cup mel-
ted butter
¼ l | ⅜ pint | 1 cup milk
2 eggs
150 g | 5 oz | 1 cup cur-
rants
90 g | 3 oz | ½ cup finely
chopped candied peel
60 g | 2 oz | ½ cup
chopped almonds

Mix together the flour, baking powder, currants, peel and almonds. Add the eggs and milk. Pour mixture into a greased floured tin and bake for 60 minutes in a moderate oven (Mark 5: 190° C/375° F). Makes 1 cake.

GARLAND CAKE Kransekake

500 g | 1 lb | 5¹/₃ cups
ground almonds
500 g | 1 lb | 3³/₄ cups
icing sugar
3 whites of egg

Mix almonds and icing sugar, and add sufficient egg white to make the mixture firm and even. Grease ring-shaped cake tins with butter, press dough through a forcing bag and place in rings. Bake in a slow oven (Mark 2: 150° C/300° F) for 20 minutes. Do not remove rings from the tins until they are cold. Place rings on top of one another to make a tower or basket. Fasten rings together with caramel sugar, pipe royal icing attractively over the cake, decorate with sweets, petits-fours and Norwegian flags. See picture.
Royal icing: – stir together *140 g | 4¹/₂ oz | 1 cup icing sugar, 1 white of egg, 1 teaspoon vinegar.* Serves 12.

NAPOLEON CAKES Napoleonskaker (Mille feuilles)

Pastry:
250 g | ¹/₂ lb | 2 cups
flour
150 g | 5 oz | ²/₃ cup
butter
4 tablespoons | ¹/₄ cup
cold water
Custard filling:
1 teaspoon vanilla
essence
2 egg yolks
40 cl | ³/₄ pint | 2 cups
cream
125 g | 4 oz | ¹/₂ cup
sugar

Rub the butter into the flour, add water, roll out the dough 1 cm | ¹/₃ inch thick. Place on a greased baking sheet, cut into strips 10 cm | 4 inches long and 3¹/₂ cm | 1¹/₂ inches wide. Bake in a moderately hot oven (Mark 3: 170° C/325° F) for 15 minutes, and cool. Place in layers of two, with custard between, and decorate with rum icing. Makes 14 cakes.

BUTTER CAKE Smørkremkake I

4 eggs
500 g | 1 lb | 2 cups
sugar
250 g | ½ lb | 2 cups
flour
1 teaspoon baking powder
buttercream
250 g | ½ lb | 1 cup
butter
140 g | 4½ oz | 1 cup
icing sugar
2 egg yolks

Beat eggs and sugar until foamy, add flour and baking powder. Bake cake in a well-greased tin for 40 minutes in a moderately hot oven (Mark 5: 190° C/375° F). Stand to cool, divide into three layers and fill with buttercream. Cover with lemon icing. Makes 1 cake.

POOR MAN'S BISCUITS Fattigmann

10 egg yolks
40 g | 1½ oz | 5 table-
spoons icing sugar
8 tablespoons | ½ cup
double cream
1 tablespoon brandy
1 teaspoon ground carda-
mom
½ teaspoon grated lemon
rind
approx. 750 g | 1½ lb | 6
cups flour
1 kg | 2 lb | 4 cups lard

Whisk egg yolks with sugar. Add stiffly whipped cream, brandy and spices. Sift in flour. Chill the dough until the next day. Roll out paperthin, cut with a pastry-cutter, and fry in lard at 180° C/350° F. Makes 84 biscuits.

FOUR-SPECIE DOLLARS Fir-spesidalere (Old family recipe)

125 g | 4 oz | 1 cup flour
250 g | ½ lb | 1 cup
butter
250 g | ½ lb | 1 cup
sugar
125 g | 4 oz | 1 cup chop-
ped blanched almonds

Sift flour, add other ingredients, knead well, shape into a round "sausage", chill until the next day. Cut with a sharp knife into thin slices. Bake for ten minutes in a moderate oven (Mark 4: 180° C/350° F). Makes 40 biscuits.

DANISH PASTRY Wienerbrød

40 cl | ¾ pint | 2 cups
lukewarm milk
2 eggs
3 tablespoons sugar
500 g | 1 lb | 4 cups flour
50 g | 1¾ oz fresh yeast
or 2 tablespoons dried
yeast (or 2 yeast cakes)
250 g | ½ lb | 1 cup
butter
almond or apple filling

Cream the yeast. Add the beaten eggs to the flour and sugar and then yeast and tepid milk. Roll out dough into an oblong shape. Spread softened butter on one half, fold the other half over it, and roll out the dough three times like flaky pastry. The dough can be shaped into a long crescent or cut into small pastries. Fill with apple filling or macaroon mixture and allow to rise for one hour. Brush with egg and bake in a moderate oven (Mark 5: 190° C/ 375° F) for half an hour. When cold, decorate with rum icing. Serves 8.

BROWN COOKIES Brune kaker

250 g | ½ lb | 1 cup melted butter
250 g | ½ lb | 1 cup sugar
175 g | 6 oz | ½ cup syrup
1 teaspoon cloves
1 tablespoon cinnamon
175 g | 6 oz | 1½ cups flour
75 g | 2½ oz | ½ cup finely chopped almonds
1 tablespoon dried bitter orange peel
1 level teaspoon sodium bicarbonate
1 tablespoon boiling water
30 blanched almonds

Heat butter, syrup and sugar in a saucepan, add spices and almonds. Dissolve the sodium bicarbonate in water, and add with flour. Let dough lie until next day, shape it into a long "sausage", and cut it into thin slices with a sharp knife. Place cakes on a greased baking sheet, sprinkle with water, decorate with halves of blanched almonds. Bake for 8–10 minutes in a slow oven (Mark 2: 150° C/ 300° F). Makes 60.

CREAM WAFFLES Rømmevafler

350 g | ³/₄ lb | 3 cups flour
³/₄ l | 1 ¹/₄ pints | 3 cups sour cream
¹/₄ l | ³/₈ pint | 1 cup cold water
250 g | ¹/₂ lb | 1 cup melted butter

Mix flour, water and butter. Whip cream stiffly and fold into the mixture. Set the dough aside for one hour. Heat waffle iron on both sides, butter lightly. Place a spoonful of dough in the iron, turn immediately. Cook waffles until golden brown on both sides, and allow to cool on a wire rack, not on top of each other. Serve with sugar and jam. Makes 16 waffles.

DALESMEN Døler

250 g | ¹/₂ lb | 1 cup sugar
250 g | ¹/₂ lb | 1 cup butter
¹/₄ l | ³/₈ pint | 1 cup double cream, whipped
150 g | 5 oz | 1 cup potato flour
250 g | ¹/₂ lb | 1 ¹/₂ cups almonds
1 teaspoon vanilla sugar

Cream the butter and sugar until white, add whipped cream, then flour, vanilla sugar and chopped blanched almonds. Spoon dough with a teaspoon on to a greased baking sheet. Bake until pale golden in a moderate oven (Mark 4: 180° C/ 350° F). Makes 50–60 small biscuits.

CHAMBERLAINS Kammerjunkere

500 g | 1 lb | 4 cups flour
125 g | 4 oz | ¹/₂ cup margarine
2 tablespoons sugar
3 eggs
40 cl | ³/₄ pint | 2 cups lukewarm milk
20 g | ³/₄ oz fresh yeast or 1 tablespoon dried yeast (or 1 yeast cake)

Cream the yeast with some of the milk. Rub the margarine into the flour and sugar. Add the yeast mixture, the eggs and milk. Work into a pliant dough and let it rise for 3 hours. Roll into small round buns. Allow to rise for one hour. Bake 15 minutes in a moderately hot oven (Mark 5: 190° C/375° F). Slice immediately and dry in a very slow oven (Mark ¹/₄: 120° C/225° F). Makes 50 rusks.

CREAM CAKE Bløtkake

5 eggs
140 g | 4¹/₂ oz | 1 cup
icing sugar
60 g | 2 oz | ¹/₂ cup flour
75 g | 2¹/₂ oz | ¹/₂ cup
potato flour
grated rind of half a lemon

Whisk the eggs with the sugar, mix in flour and potato flour, add the lemon rind and pour into a round well-greased cake tin. Bake for 30 minutes in a moderate oven (Mark 4: 180° C/350° F). Allow to cool, divide into three layers, drench each layer with home-made wine or sherry.

Filling:
whipped cream and strawberry jam, or walnut cream
vanilla custard
Decorate with:
cream, fresh or deep-frozen strawberries
marzipan, walnut halves
chocolate icing
etc.

Fill a few hours before serving to bring out the full flavour. Serves 10–12.

GORO Goro

2 eggs
750 g | 1¹/₂ lb | 3 cups
sugar
1 tablespoon vanilla sugar
40 cl | ³/₄ pint | 2 cups
double cream
1 glass brandy
¹/₂ teaspoon ground cardamom
¹/₂ teaspoon grated lemon rind
600 g | 1¹/₄ lb | 2¹/₂ cups
butter
about 1¹/₂ kg | 3 lb | 12 cups flour

Beat eggs and sugar, add stiffly whipped cream, brandy and spices. Knead in butter and flour alternately. Do not use all the flour, but save a little for rolling out. Let dough stand for 24 hours. Roll out as thinly as possible. Cook cakes until golden brown in a goro iron.

SAND CAKE Sandkake

500 g | 1 lb | 2¼ cups
castor sugar
500 g | 1 lb | 2 cups
butter
6 eggs
250 g | ½ lb | 2 cups
flour
250 g | ½ lb | 1½ cups
potato flour
2 teaspoons baking
powder
grated rind of one lemon

Cream the butter and sugar until white, add the egg yolks, sift in the flour, potato flour and baking powder, then the lemon rind and stiffly beaten egg whites. Put the mixture into two well-greased tins and bake for 60 minutes in a hot oven (Mark 6: 200° C/400° F). Makes 2 cakes.

SERINA BISCUITS Serinakaker

500 g | 1 lb | 4 cups flour
400 g | 14 oz | 2 cups
castor sugar
500 g | 1 lb | 2 cups
butter
2 eggs
60 g | 2 oz | ½ cup
almonds
1½ teaspoons baking
powder
4 teaspoons vanilla sugar

Mix the flour with the baking powder, rub in the cold butter and add the egg yolks, and one egg white whisked up with sugar and vanilla. Shape the dough into small balls, flatten slightly with a fork, brush with white of egg and sprinkle with chopped blanched almonds. Bake until golden brown in a moderate oven (Mark 4: 180° C/ 350° F) for 12 minutes. Makes 60.

BUTTERCREAM CAKE Smørkremkake II.

40 g | 1½ oz | 3 table-
spoons butter
275 g | 9 oz | 2 cups
icing sugar
20 g | ¾ oz | 3 table-
spoons cocoa
1 teaspoon vanilla sugar
8 tablespoons | ½ cup
strong coffee
sponge cake

Mix all ingredients and cream together until smooth. Divide a plain sponge cake into layers. Place one layer on the dish, spread with buttercream, place a chocolate or coffee cake of the same size on top, and spread with cream. Then place the other sponge layer on top. Decorate with chocolate icing. Serves 12.

RUSKS Kavringer

*500 g | 1 lb | 4 cups
wheat flour
500 g | 1 lb | 4 cups rye
flour
2 teaspoons salt
250 g | 1/2 lb | 1 cup
butter
50 g | 1 1/2 oz fresh yeast
or 2 tablespoons dried
yeast (or 2 yeast cakes)
3/4 l | 1 1/4 pints | 3 cups
lukewarm water*

Cream the yeast with a little of the water. Mix the salt, sugar and flour, add water and the yeast mixture and work into a fairly soft dough. Allow to stand in a cool spot 24 hours. Add butter cold, work the dough once more and roll out to finger thickness. Divide into circles with an inverted glass and bake in a moderate oven (Mark 5: 190° C/375° F) for 30 minutes. Cut with sharp knife and dry in a very slow oven (Mark 1/4: 120° C/225° F) until quite crisp. Makes about 40.

Sandwiches

Smørbrød

Scandinavia's own single-decker version of the sandwich.

That sandwiches are no more food
Than love and hate are of one mood
Is all I know and all I write
Of love and sandwiches tonight.

Thus sang a Norwegian poet, Johan Herman Wessel, nearly two centuries ago. Much has happened since then, and today sandwiches have established themselves as food fit for the faddiest fancier of fine fare and fodder, thanks not least to the renaissance that the sandwich has enjoyed in Scandinavia. Today, in Scandinavia at least, the sandwich is no longer an interloper among dishes, a pinchbeck snack skulking between protective slabs of bread, lying in ambush for the unwary, a snare and a delusion to the self-respecting palate. No, the sandwich in Scandinavia – or smørbrød if you like, for the rose by any other name will smell as sweet – has come out into the open, and merely nestles coyly on a single sliver of bread.

Norwegian sandwiches are renowned for their tempting appearance and succulence. But then, Norwegian sandwich-makers set about their task with the reverence and care which your genuine smørbrød demands. The bread must be cut to the right thickness, the butter must be soft enough to spread evenly over its surface, while the actual "spread" must be fresh and alluring and never give an impression of overcrowding.

There are, of course, endless varieties. Here are a number of outstanding examples, chosen because of the appeal they make to visitors to Norway.

BIRD SONG Fuglesang

4 slices bread
4 slices boiled ham
1 raw chopped onion
4 raw egg yolks
1 bunch chives, finely chopped

Chop the ham, mix with the onion, and spread on buttered bread. Make a depression in each, and pour in an egg yolk. Sprinkle with chives. Serves 4.

BEEF TARTARE Biff tartar

4 raw egg yolks
1 teaspoon salt
1 pinch pepper
4 slices white bread
butter
2 tablespoons chopped
parsley
500 g | 1 lb beef
2 tablespoons chopped
raw onion
2 tablespoons chopped
pickled beetroot
2 tablespoons capers

Scrape beef, or put once through mincer, divide into four and spread evenly on the buttered bread. Garnish with onion, beetroot, capers and parsley, and serve with yolks of egg, each contained in its shell, in the middle of each piece. Sprinkle with pepper and salt. Serves 4.

CROWN PRINCESS MÄRTHA'S SPECIAL SANDWICH Kronprinsesse Märthas spesialsmørbrød

4 slices white bread
butter
500 g | 1 lb freshly boiled
cod's roes
8 tablespoons | ½ cup
thick béchamel sauce with
finely chopped dill
150 g | 5 oz | 1 cup
peeled prawns

Cut cod's roes into small pieces less than 1 cm | ½ inch thick. Fry lightly in butter and place piping hot on a slice of buttered bread. Pour warm béchamel-dill sauce on top, and sprinkle with prawns. Serves 4.

SMOKED EEL SANDWICH Smørbrød med røket ål

4 slices bread
butter
8 pieces smoked eel
scrambled egg
fresh watercress

Place a strip of scrambled egg, with a piece of smoked eel on either side on each slice of buttered bread. Garnish with fresh watercress. Serves 4.

GENTLEMEN'S SPECIAL Herrens spesial

8 slices bread
4 slices boiled ham
4 slices gruyère
butter

Remove the crusts from the slices of bread and spread each slice evenly with butter. Place a slice of ham on one slice of bread, and a piece of cheese on the other, and sandwich the two together, bread on the outside. Fry in butter until the bread is crisp, and the cheese is oozing out. Serves 4.

"BULL'S EYE" Okseøye

4 slices bread
butter
4 egg yolks
4 slivers onion
8 filleted anchovies
2 teaspoons capers
fresh watercress

Cut out a large round from each slice of bread. Spread the rounds with butter. Drape the anchovy fillets round the edge of each circle of bread. Place a ring of onion inside, a raw egg yolk in the middle, with capers sprinkled round it. Garnish the serving dish with watercress. Serves 4.

COD'S ROE SANDWICH Torskerognsmørbrød

4 slices bread
butter
8 slices warm fried cod's roe
4 slices lemon
1 tube mayonnaise

Place the warm roe on the buttered bread. Garnish with a slice of lemon, and squeeze a little mayonnaise round the roe. Serves 4.

THE VET'S NIGHTCAP Dyrlegens nattmat

4 slices bread
3 tablespoons dripping (or butter)
4 thick slices home-made liver paste
4 slivers aspic jelly
4 slices cured meat

Spread the dripping evenly on the bread, cover with liver paste. Garnish with aspic jelly and thin slices of cured meat. Serves 4.

LAND IN SIGHT Landgang

4 long slices bread, cut
lengthwise from a sand-
wich (or tin) loaf
butter
4 slices smoked salmon
75 g | 2¹/2 oz | ¹/2 cup
peeled prawns
1 tube mayonnaise
2 hard-boiled eggs
4 slices boiled ham
1 tomato
chopped parsley
4 slices cheese
4 radishes

Butter the bread and divide into four
equal areas. On the first place
smoked salmon and prawns garnished with mayonnaise, on the second slices of hard-boiled egg and
tomato sprinkled with parsley, on the
third rolls of boiled ham, and on the
fourth cheese and finely chopped
radish. Serves 4.

FRIED FISH FILLET Smørbrød med stekt fiskefilet

4 slices bread
butter
4 crisply fried warm fish
fillets
fresh lemon
parsley
remoulade sauce

Place the warm fish fillets on the
buttered bread and garnish with lemon and parsley. Serve with remoulade sauce. Enough for 4.

HAM-AND-EGG SANDWICH Patentsmørbrød

4 slices bread
1 tablespoon butter
4 slices boiled ham
4 eggs

Butter the bread, grill the ham lightly,
and fry the eggs. Place a slice of
grilled ham and a warm fried egg on
each slice of bread. Serves 4.

PRAWNS ON THE ROCKS Rekesmørbrød

4 slices bread
butter
300 g | 10 oz | 2 cups
freshly peeled prawns
mayonnaise
4 lemon slices
4 parsley sprigs

Butter the bread, and arrange the
prawns pyramid-fashion on top of it.
Garnish with mayonnaise, lemon and
parsley. Serves 4.

HOT CHEESE SANDWICH Varmt ostesmørbrød

4 slices bread
1 tablespoon butter
1 1/2 teaspoons mustard
4 pieces gruyère cheese

Stir mustard and butter together, spread evenly on bread and cover with a piece of gruyère cheese. Heat under a hot grill until the cheese has melted and started to brown. Serve piping hot. Serves 4.

HAM SANDWICH Smørbrød med skinke

4 slices bread
butter
4 slices boiled ham
4 tablespoons Italian salad
thin slices cucumber
parsley

Place a slice of ham in the shape of a cornet on each slice of buttered bread. Fill each cornet with Italian salad, and garnish with cucumber and parsley. Serves 4.

KIRSTEN FLAGSTAD'S FAVOURITE SANDWICH Kirsten Flagstads favorittsmørbrød
Kidney en croute

1/2 ox-kidney
plain flour for dusting
salt and pepper
6 tablespoons butter
1/4 l | 3/8 pint | 1 cup single cream
1 glass sherry
4 slices milk bread
4 slices cooked celeriac
4 slices baked apple

Garnish:
4 tomato slices
4 parsley sprigs

Cut up half an ox-kidney into small cubes, dust with flour, salt and pepper and brown in 1 1/2 tablespoon of the butter. Add 1/4 l | 3/8 pint | 1 cup cream and one glass of sherry and simmer for 5 minutes. Remove crust from four slices of milk loaf and fry in butter. Place one round, lightly boiled disc of celeriac on each slice, then a warm, thick slice of baked apple. Spoon the kidney on top of each croute and garnish with tomato and parsley. Serves 4.

Fruit Juices, Jams and Preserves

There is hardly a patch of garden in the whole of Norway which does not produce a little rhubarb, or contain a few blackcurrant or redcurrant bushes, and a few apple trees. Fruit and berries are very popular in Norway, and the Norwegian housewife uses a great variety of fruit preparations in her kitchen. In fact, a cellar full of such preserves is a Norwegian housewife's pride.

APPLE JELLY Eplegelé

2 kg | 4 lb unripe cooking apples
90 cl | 1½ pints (1 U.S. quart) water
3 kg | 6 lb | 12 cups sugar

Wash apples (but do not peel), quarter, and boil to a soft mush in just enough water to cover them. Stand for 25 minutes, strain and measure. Add 500 g | 1 lb sugar for every 60 cl | 1 pint of juice. Simmer 8–10 minutes, skim carefully, and place in small clean jars. Makes 3 kg | 6 lb of stiff jelly.

CHERRY JAM Kirsebærsyltetøy

500 g | 1 lb stoned cherries
500 g | 1 lb | 2 cups sugar
½ vanilla pod

Remove stones from large cooking cherries, sprinkle with sugar and stand until next day. Boil for 20 minutes with the vanilla pod. Crush some of the stones, add kernels and stand for 25 minutes. Strain off juice, boil briskly and pour hot over berries. Store the jam in a cold place.

RED WHORTLEBERRY JAM Tyttebærsyltetøy

1 kg | 2 lb red whortle-
berries
500 g | 1 lb | 2 cups
sugar
1/2 vanilla pod

Clean berries, boil half of them with sugar for 15 minutes, remove and add the rest of the berries. Stir until cold, put into jars and seal.

GRANDMA'S BAKED PLUMS Bestemors bakte plommer

1 kg | 2 lb Victoria plums
500 g | 1 lb | 2 cups
sugar
8 tablespoons | 1/2 cup
Jamaica rum

Wash plums, prick with a needle, and place in a fireproof jug in layers. Sprinkle sugar between each layer. Pour rum over. Place jug in a moderate oven (Mark 4: 180° C/350° F) for 45 minutes, switch off the heat and allow the plums to cool in oven.

KING OSCAR II'S FAVOURITE JAM Kong Oscars favorittsyltetøy

1 kg | 2 lb blackcurrants
1 1/2 l | 2 1/2 pints | 6 cups
water
1 kg | 2 lb | 4 cups sugar

Avoid over-ripe berries or the jam will not set properly. Clean, rinse and put into a wide-necked jar with the water. Place the jar in water and cook until the berries soften. Stand until next day. Strain, boil for 10 minutes with sugar, skim, and place in dry, warm jars. Seal immediately.

PICKLES Pickles

100 small cucumbers
(gherkins)
1 cauliflower
175 g | 6 oz | 1 cup
green peas
3 small pickling onions,
peeled
1 teaspoon ground nut-
meg
1 teaspoon whole yellow
mustard seeds
1 small Spanish pepper
(chili)
90 cl | 1½ pints | 4 cups
vinegar
250 g | ½ lb | 1 cup
sugar
fresh sprigs dill

Wash the cucumbers and place for one day in brine (250 g | ½ lb | 1 cup salt to 1½ l | 2½ pints | 6 cups water). Remove, dry and place in jars in layers with parboiled sprigs of cauliflower, the onions and peas. Boil vinegar, sugar and spices, and pour over whilst hot. Garnish with dill.

STRAWBERRY JAM Jordbærsyltetøy (from grandmother's cookery book)

500 g | 1 lb | 3¼ cups
strawberries
500 g | 1 lb | 2 cups
sugar
4 tablespoons | ¼ cup
brandy

Clean and rinse the strawberries, place in a saucepan with sugar. Allow to stand for 24 hours and then boil slowly, until clear and soft. Boil the syrup for 12 minutes, replace berries and boil for a further 2 minutes. Skim, take off boil and add brandy. Ladle out syrup into clean jars which have been rinsed with brandy.

STIRRED RASPBERRIES Rørte bringebær

1 kg | 2 lb raspberries
1 kg | 2 lb | 4 cups sugar
8 tablespoons | ½ cup
cognac

Clean the berries, sprinkle with sugar, add cognac, and stir the preserve slowly for half an hour.

PICKLED BEETROOT Syltede rødbeter

1 kg | 2 lb beetroots
water
3/4 l | 1¼ pints | 3 cups vinegar
125 g | 4 oz | ½ cup sugar
1 teaspoon caraway seeds

Wash the beetroots but do not peel. Boil in lightly salted water in a large saucepan until just tender. Do not prick the beetroots while boiling, or they will 'bleed'. Peel and slice thinly with a vegetable knife, place in a jar with a little caraway between each layer. Boil vinegar and sugar and pour piping hot over the beetroots. Ready after 14 days.

UNCOOKED RASPBERRY JUICE Rå bringebærsaft

1 kg | 2 lb raspberries
1½ l | 2½ pints | 6 cups water
10 g tartaric acid crystals
sugar

Clean and crush berries. Pour cold boiled water over them. Dissolve tartaric acid in warm water and pour over. Let berries stand for 24 hours, strain off juice and stand for another 24 hours. Add 500 g | 1 lb | 2 cups sugar to each 1¼ l | 1 quart | 5 cups of juice, stir until the sugar dissolves, pour into dry, clean jars, and seal with greaseproof paper.

STIRRED RED WHORTLEBERRIES Rørte tyttebær

1 kg | 2 lb red whortle-berries
1 kg | 2 lb | 4 cups sugar

Clean the berries and place in a dish with the sugar. Stir slowly in same direction for at least an hour, preferably two, or 15 minutes in a food mixer. Put the jam into jars and seal, but stir each week.

87

"Odds and Ends"

BURNT ALMONDS Brente mandler

500 g | 1 lb | 3 cups blanched almonds 500 g | 1 lb | 2 cups sugar 3/4 l | 1 1/4 pints | 3 cups water 3 tablespoons butter	Boil the almonds with the sugar and water. Stir constantly until all the water has evaporated. Remove the pan from the heat, but stir for another five minutes. Add butter, bring to the boil again until sugar is browned. Tip the almonds onto a buttered china dish, and separate them while still warm.

ANCHOVY COCKTAIL Ansjoscocktail

12 anchovies 4 teaspoons finely chopped raw onion 2 teaspoons capers 4 egg yolks watercress	Take four cocktail glasses. Clean the anchovies, chop them finely and divide among the glasses. Sprinkle with onion and capers. Place a raw egg yolk carefully on top of each. Garnish with watercress. Serves 4.

CHERRY MAID Kirsebær-cocktail

90 cl | 1 1/2 pints | 4 cups cherry juice 500 g | 1 lb | 2 cups sugar 1 teaspoon citric acid 2 drops almond essence 1 teaspoon vanilla sugar	Boil together the juice and sugar, cool, add dissolved citric acid, then the vanilla sugar and almonds. Shake well, serve with crushed ice.

CREAM CARAMELS Fløtekarameller

40 cl | ³/4 pint | 2 cups cream
500 g | 1 lb | 2 cups sugar
175 g | 6 oz | ¹/2 cup golden syrup
1 tablespoon cocoa
1 tablespoon butter

Mix all the ingredients in a heavy saucepan and heat gently until viscous. Pour into a greased square tin. Cut into squares and separate when cool.

EGGNOG VIKING Eggedosis

10 egg yolks
150 g | 5 oz | 10 tablespoons sugar

Whisk the egg yolks and sugar thoroughly with a wire whisk, a rotary beater or an electric whisk until the mixture is foamy. Serve immediately in sundae glasses, adding one teaspoon of brandy to each glass. Traditional for May 17th, Norway's Independence Day. Serves 6.

GRANNY'S COUGH CURE Bestemors hostesaft

2 eggs, in their shells
1 sliced lemon
500 g | 1 lb | 2 cups sugar
¹/2 bottle Jamaica rum

Place the eggs in a bowl, cover with lemon slices. Allow to stand for 24 hours. Crush the eggs, press and strain them through a cloth, then stir in rum and sugar.

MARZIPAN Marsipan

500 g | 1 lb | 5¹/3 cups ground almonds
500 g | 1 lb | 3¹/2 cups icing sugar
3 egg whites

Knead sugar, almonds and egg whites into a pliable dough. Can be used as sweetmeats, in cakes, or as decorations, shaped into flowers or fruit and coloured with confectioner's colouring. Marzipan pigs are very popular in Norway at Christmas time.

COCKTAIL CANAPES Pinnemat

Cut thin circles of white bread about 3 to 4 cm | 1½ inches in diameter. Garnish temptingly, with for example:
Caviar inside a border of sieved, hard-boiled egg yolk or a ring of hard-boiled egg white; mussel with lemon sliver; smoked salmon roll with sprig of dill; three prawns with parsley; piquant cheese with mustard; olives stuffed with paprika. Place on a flat dish. Spear the bite-sized savouries with cocktail sticks.

SALTED ALMONDS Salte mandler

Fry 175 g | 6 oz | 1 cup blanched almonds in lard, drain on kitchen paper and sprinkle with salt.

SALT TWIGLETS Salte pinner

250 g | ½ lb | 2 cups flour
250 g | ½ lb | 1 cup butter
1½ teaspoons baking powder
1 heaped teaspoon salt
¼ l | ⅜ pint | 1 cup cream
beaten egg yolk for glazing

Rub the butter into the flour, add the salt and baking powder. Blend the mixture with the cream, knead into a dough, and set aside for one hour. Roll out into thin sticks, brush with egg and sprinkle with salt. Bake until crisp and golden brown in a moderate oven (Mark 4: 180° C/350° F) for 12 minutes. Serve hot with cocktails, or to accompany soup.

ENGLISH RECIPE INDEX

NORWEGIAN RECIPE INDEX

GLOSSARY OF TERMS

English	American equivalent or substitute
Beetroot(s)	beet(s)
castor sugar	superfine granulated sugar
cornflour	cornstarch
double cream	heavy cream
essence (e.g. vanilla)	extract
fry (in shallow fat)	panfry
frying pan	skillet
girdle	griddle
greaseproof paper	wax paper
grill	broiler
icing sugar	confectioner's sugar
jar (for preserves)	jelly glass or cup
kitchen paper	paper towel
minced	ground
pinch	dash
plain flour	all-purpose flour
prawn(s)	shrimp
royal icing	sugar frosting
single cream	light cream
tin (for cake-making)	form

Editor's note:
Anchovies are among the ingredients in a number of recipes in this book. Scandinavian 'anchovies' should be used in preference to those from the Mediterranean.